Additional Praise for *Coast Range*

"A well-timed debut that transports readers to the coastal ranges of California and Oregon and fully immerses them in the natural and cultural history of the Pacific Northwest's cobbled beaches, ice-cold rivers, pine canopies, and layered forest floors . . . Neely's skill with language is evident throughout. What makes Neely's collection so compelling is the detail, his artful engagement of our senses to feel the weight of the agate, taste the flake of the fish, trace the letters carved into the madrone trees, and then smell the sour decay of atonement and fall in love with this place."

—*Orion*

"In Nick Neely's new book, *Coast Range: A Collection from the Pacific Edge*, he aptly captures that childlike sense of wonder about the natural world . . . The essays are just as pleasant to read for his meticulously arranged prose and artfully crafted imagery as they are for their educational qualities."

—*Idaho Mountain Express*

"Nick Neely is a searcher and, lucky for us, a collector as well. *Coast Range* is his collection, his 'open-air curiosity cabinet,' full of newts, agates, madrones, mushrooms, coyote, salmon, paw prints, bones and beautiful sentences. He is a precise writer and his essays are brilliant in the shining sense. But as well as being an accurate observer of the natural world, he is an exuberant participant, and we are both pulled in and lifted up by his generous, buoyant, and ever-curious spirit. An important book, and one full of life and joy."

—DAVID GESSNER, author of *All the Wild That Remains* and *Sick of Nature*

"I don't know if 'God is in the detail,' as the saying goes, but I think much of nature is. Nick Neely's *Coast Range* is an erudite, eloquent demonstration of that, from the vividly evoked details of ancient mollusks scraping their way into rocks to those of even more ancient fungi lacing themselves into tree roots . . . Neely's vigilant, wry commentaries on his native patch of the west coast are not only in the tradition of Thoreau's *Walden* but in an older and wider one that he shares with Thoreau: what Thoreau calls 'the great dragon-tree' of mythic vision that is associated with Homer and Sophocles but also lives in Aristotle, Herodotus, Pliny, and other classical naturalists."

—DAVID RAINES WALLACE, author of *Mountains and Marshes*
and *The Untamed Garden*

"Neely's fascination with a huge swath of the Pacific Northwest coastal range is evident in this quiet essay collection that focuses on small details described in carefully studied prose . . . This is the sort of introspective writing that will appeal strongly to readers seeking to gain a deeper appreciation of their environment, and those with curiosity about or longing for the region he knows so well. Neely clearly spent a lot of time watching and listening, both to the people and animals that call the area home, and his observations have real staying power."

—*Booklist*

"Fans of Joseph Wood Krutch, Henry David Thoreau, and John Muir will enjoy these essays even if they are not familiar with the specific geographic area."

—*Library Journal*

"I hate nature essays, but I like Nick Neely's nature essays. That's because while there's nature here, he doesn't default to reverence in the face of the sublime; he doesn't crow about conservation or bore us with rhapsodies of trees. Instead he's drawn to people, weirdos, and obsessives like himself: homesteaders, trappers, buffet captains, game wardens, biologists, and duchesses. This book's an obsessive and glorious cataloging of the natural world and its effects: how it changes us and is changed by us. *Coast Range* suggests that to look is to collect, the most noble of pursuits, and by so doing, 'to hold, and possibly hoard, the world.' Look hard enough and long enough at anything, he seems to tell us, and we lose ourselves, which is a kind of love."

—ANDER MONSON, author of *Neck Deep*
and *Letter to a Future Lover*

Coast Range

A Collection from the Pacific Edge

NICK NEELY

COUNTERPOINT | BERKELEY

For my parents

For Sarah

Copyright © 2016 by Nick Neely

All rights reserved under International and Pan-American Copyright
Conventions. No part of this book may be used or reproduced in any manner
whatsoever without written permission from the publisher, except in the case
of brief quotations embodied in critical articles and reviews.

Paperback ISBN: 978-1-64009-013-2

The Library of Congress has cataloged the hardcover as follows:
Names: Neely, Nick, author.
Title: Coast range : a collection from the Pacific edge / Nick Neely.
Description: Berkeley : Counterpoint Press, [2016]
Identifiers: LCCN 2016020226 | ISBN 9781619028364 (hardback)
Subjects: LCSH: Neely, Nick. | BISAC: NATURE / Essays.
Classification: LCC AC8 .N35 2016 | DDC 979--dc23
LC record available at https://lccn.loc.gov/2016020226

Cover design by Debbie Berne
Interior design by Neuwirth & Associates

COUNTERPOINT
2560 Ninth Street, Suite 318
Berkeley, CA 94710
www.counterpointpress.com

Printed in the United States of America
Distributed by Publishers Group West

1 3 5 7 9 10 8 6 4 2

Contents

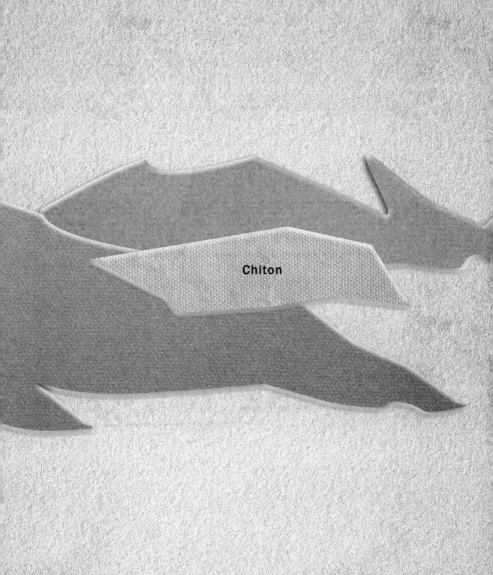

Chiton

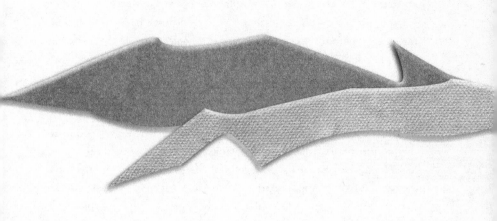

Along my home California coast, you may find, on the softest littoral rock, an infinite number of subtle dimples. It's as if, for eons, some ambitious soul lingered to rub first this spot, then that, until each became a smooth and nearly uniform divot. These shallow holes—catching seawater, reflecting sky and fog—are not the work of some invisible thumb, however, but of the foot of a five-hundred-million-year-old: a mollusk. They are the resting places of chiton.

Now the best way to understand a chiton (kī-tän) is to wait until sunset, flop on your belly at the sea's rocky edge, and lie quite still. Make sure it's high tide, when chitons are busiest. Then, with your ear pressed to the stone, you might hear the faint vibrations of scraping as, underwater, their rasp-like radulae rev up in their mouths and they begin to lurch forward to graze the algal fields, inch by inch. Some chitons reap "diatom scuzz"; others prefer a healthy leaf of algae. All cut with precision: The outermost "teeth" of their radulae are capped with magnetite, harder than stainless steel.

Chitons are also called "sea cradles," because eight calcareous plates overlap across their backs, a defensive arch surrounded by a fleshy girdle. More than nine hundred species crawl the world's shores, but they're most varied on our West Coast (and in Australia). If you're lucky, while perusing a Pacific tide pool you might chance upon a foot-long brick-red gumboot chiton, a creature lovingly nicknamed the "wandering meatloaf." This giant's leathery girdle actually wraps clear around its plates and is slightly fuzzy to the touch: Twenty species of red algae grow on its back. All of which makes me wonder if the gumboot wouldn't enjoy nibbling on itself, just a little.

Chitons are guarded, territorial. They don't like limpets, another grazer. They have light-sensitive organs, "aesthetes," in their shells—their plates are innervated—which relay signals to the region resembling a head. Some even have lens-bearing "eyes" on their backs and see shapes. Thus, when your shadow crosses, a chiton will cling fast, masquerading as rock. Should you, or a wave, catch and flip a chiton upside down by surprise, however, it will curl into a tectonic ball and go with the flow, tumbling to safety.

But this is why it's really worth lying on your stomach: Each night, some chiton species creep forward on established trails to their feeding grounds, usually no more than a few feet from their primary dimple. Out and back, they go, harvesting, and by morning return on these mucal routes to their hammocks in the stone, where they seal tight to conserve moisture. They perform these rounds for months before moving on to fresh algal pastures. Do you hear them? No one knows how they navigate, exactly, nor how they scour their pits (and some species don't).

Like limpets, their secretions may dissolve the stone, before they polish off the job with their teeth. But now, again, I find myself wondering: Is the chiton's home its groove, equally a rut and a cradle? Or is it the endless forays made from this center?

The Book of Agate

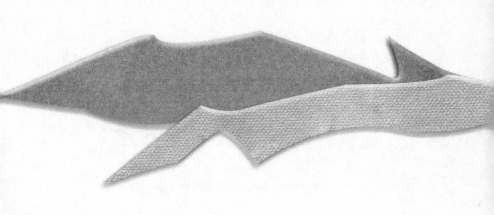

Here, on my desk, lies a handful of beach agates, catching the winter light. They are charms I've given myself to play with. Comforts, pacifiers. Curiosities.

Some are smooth, buttery, worn round by water and time; others are angular and rough, perhaps removed too soon from their wash cycle.

But even these, I find, are easy on the fingers.

Recently these stones—mostly small, translucent pebbles—were lodged in the silt of a river delta, but now they are clean and dry, preserved for a spell. They've found a home.

Once an object joins a collection, it tends to become more than itself. Not just symbolic, but sacred. It is retired from all former use, if there was any in its previous incarnation.

Then even a stone snatched from the multitudes—one that's caromed for thousands of years without much consequence—can no longer be handled so lightly.

Dropping one to the floor, I can't help but wince a little.

Something collected recalls its many origins all at once: layers of association difficult to distinguish, let alone describe, amid that warm feeling of general owner's satisfaction.

Holding up this milky pebble to look within, I seem to confront an immeasurable history compressed into an object.

Not just the white lines barreling in on the beach where this rock was discovered—waves that crash down even now, thousands of miles away—but also the eroded pocket in the hills from which it came and every scouring riffle in between.

Agates gather in darkness, in lava rock, where silica gradually precipitates from groundwater. In ancient bubbles and faults, a gel forms, and as it dehydrates, the incipient crystal separates into discrete but fused bands. Eventually, the emptiness of the cavity is filled with a seamless quartz known as chalcedony.

If a small cave is left at the center, then your agate is in fact a geode, a word that means "earthy," though those glittering innards may seem more like ice or air.

Agate nodules come in all shapes, sizes, colors, and degrees of translucence: from granule to boulder, vermilion to cerulean, clear to opaque. Depends on their original mold, the mineral content of their natal waters, and other mysteries.

So it was that, millions of year ago, these agates began to come into my life.

But I remember, also, that June day when my love and I drove west from Eugene on a misty road, past pastures and barns and clear-cuts on the Douglas fir hillsides.

How we hung a right on Highway 101, curving through dunes and over headlands, until, from the precipitous heights of Cape Perpetua, we descended to a town far from anywhere and clinging to the shore: *Welcome to Yachats: The Gem of the Oregon Coast*. Pop. 600.

In the Chinook language, Yachats (yah-hots) means "dark waters at the foot of the mountain." Just before town, we drove across the modest river, slow and tannic, overhung with maple and alder. Waters flowing out of the mossy Coast Range into a shallow bay.

All my life, it seems, I have collected places, looking, I suspect, for just the right one. Here in the Northwest was a pocket in which our eyes felt suddenly comfortable.

Yachats is all edges—mountains meeting river, meeting ocean, meeting sky—but ideally proportioned, charming, as if it would all fit beneath the dome of a snow globe.

Turn over these stones, and thoughts flurry.

As a child, I was given a small red plastic rock tumbler one Christmas, because I had the collecting bug: the impulse to hold, and possibly hoard, the world.

Or rather, it had collected me.

A tumbler mimics water. As the drum slowly rotates, it piles rock on top of rock, over and over. First harsh sand is added, and then polishing powder, so that, when the grinding is over and all is quiet, each stone shines like water itself.

Below the surface of our backyard, however, I found only crumbly sandstone, too soft to polish. So I had to look elsewhere for gems: In wildflowers. Flitting through oaks.

Spotted salamanders, glistening under pots.

Books.

Collections, I've read, often begin with a gift or serendipity. Rarely are they planned. But once that first item is in hand, others accrue as if by their own volition.

John Dewey: "No unprejudiced observer will lightly deny the existence of an original tendency to assimilate objects and events to the self, to make them part of the 'me.' We may even admit that the 'me' cannot exist without the 'mine.' The self gets solidity and form through an appropriation of things which identifies them with whatever we call myself. . . . 'I own therefore I am.'"

Solidity and form: A collection is the silica that gradually fills some part of the psyche.

Usually my Yachats agates rest in a glass bowl, but sometimes I find them scattered across my desk, among my papers and receipts. Lately they sit in clusters on stacks of unread books as if to prevent me from working.

"I am unpacking my library," wrote Walter Benjamin. "Yes, I am."

Suddenly emboldened, I sweep them into the cup of my hand, let them go clinking back into their dish. There, I can keep an eye on them.

Such are the gentle tides of a rare day.

"Guard well your spare moments," wrote Emerson. "They are like uncut diamonds. Discard them and their value will never be known. Improve them and they will become the brightest gems in a useful life."

The truth is diamonds are a dull choice: They serve as currency because none can be told apart. Nor are they actually rare. The market is only carefully controlled, and advertised.

No two agates are alike in design, and each has a chemical fingerprint, sometimes plainly visible, that an expert can trace to within fifty miles of its source.

The philosopher Theophrastus (372–287 B.C.), a disciple of Aristotle, was the first to write of agates in his treatise *On Stones*. "The *achates* is also a beautiful stone," he wrote, "it comes from the river Achates in Sicily and is sold at a high price."

Fidus Achates, friend of Aeneas.

But agates in fact come tumbling down streams and mountains the world over, and today are considered only semiprecious.

"Semi-worthless," goes the joke.

Some of these rocks can offer a view, though, not unlike a kaleidoscope; a toy that, now that I think of it, houses bits of glass like those gleaned from a beach.

A word that comes from the Greek *kalos*, "beautiful," and *eidos*, "form."

Turn the tube, faintly hear the sound of the sea within.

We checked into the Dublin House motel, ended up staying three days. The woman at the rock shop down the street showed us several sample agates in a basket, whetting my appetite.

Below the highway, in the placid Yachats River channel, a giant log was beached like a whale, saplings and long grass spouting from its weathered back.

At low tide, we walked across the sand to dip our hands into the brackish water and found evidence that a forest had once lined the stream: the octopoid roots of trees knocked over by a rising sea, a sudden tidal wave, or a more recent wave of settlers.

Remnants, excavated by the same winter storms that bring agates to light.

At first my love hunted gamely with me. But she had no luck and, before long, gave up and sat down on a stump. She might tell it differently.

There, at her feet, she found an orange agate—I could hardly believe it—and, satisfied, went off to paint the landscape for which she has infinite patience.

My nature is to keep searching.

It's believed that agate separates into bands because of electrical charges and slight chemical variations. Often these strata include mineral impurities of vivid color, iron oxides especially, blues and reds.

When cut or polished, an agate's surface has striations that resemble tree rings, as if one could count back the years to see when drought occurred and civilizations fell.

Petrified wood is also agatized, each fibrous cell replaced by silica. In my bowl are several old-growth stones, which are common along the Oregon coast. Each is a piece of tanbark from a lost playground.

Inside the chamber of a developing agate, gravity sometimes pulls the chalcedony to the floor, forming a pool of horizontal layers called "onyx," which means "fingernail."

Expose these glassy interiors, and one can see entire landscapes: Anvil-head clouds hanging over desert buttes. Whitecaps to the horizon.

Turning my index finger in the window's light, the fine keratinous ridges of my fingernail remind me of breakers as seen from a headland.

Pliny the Elder also wrote at length of agate in his *Natural History*, describing many varieties: "The Indian agate . . . on them you will find represented rivers, woods, and farm horses; and one can see in them coaches, small chariots, and horse litters and in addition the fittings and trappings of horses. . . . Those found in Thrace and near the mountain Oeta, upon Mount Parnassus, on the isle of Lesbos and in Messene, have the image of flowers, such as grow in the highways and paths in the fields."

I'm new at agate-gazing, but so far haven't encountered any equines.

As we drove along the Oregon coast, we were absorbed by the bands of the landscape: The blue and white waves. The slick and dry stretches of sand. The quiet back pools reflecting the fast clouds off the Pacific.

⌐⌐‿⌐⌐

Swaths of tidal marsh. Bluffs and chasms. The pavement the thinnest of lines.

Wreathes of beach cobble, too many stones to fathom. Mountains.

Holding this one, I remember how islands rose out of the sea, and how lava flowed into the ocean in a hissing swirl of steam, leaving hills of lumpish pillow basalt.

How the Juan de Fuca plate offshore collided with the North American plate, lifting the entire smoldering mass between sixty-six million and thirty-six million years ago, forming the Coast Range and this gorgeous drive.

This layer of continent is now disappearing: Sea stacks stand as pillars to a former coastline, and the basalt of the shore is riddled with coves and inlets that funnel waves furiously into blowholes, as if in homage to a volcanic past and the migrating gray whales.

Cruelly, the coast dumps its agates directly in the sea. But I have salvaged a few.

Whenever I'm distracted, one of these agates tends to find its way into my hands, turning over, and over, as if in an eddy. It seems to look into me.

Here I hold an opaque blue agate, one of my best. Slightly wider than my thumb, but shorter, it has what seems a wart on its pale bottom. That, or the dark eye of a hurricane.

Many agates do have "eyes." These are thought to form when stalactites or burls of chalcedony, hanging from the rind of an unfinished agate, are enveloped by more crystallization. When the agate is eventually worn or cut, spots stare out.

The other side of this blue stone has a groove that reminds me of a narrow lake surrounded by elevated terraces, or a reservoir with bathtub rings along its tiny shoreline.

How I found this blue agate I can no longer quite recall. The minute I did, my mind filled with excitement and scattered. I wanted to show her this keepsake up on the bluff.

But I think I was on my knees, and by writing this line, I make it so.

It's true that people become hesitant to collect after childhood for fear of being seen as simpleminded or self-indulgent. Unproductive.

To engage with rocks is a pretty silly business.

Annie Dillard tells of a man on the Washington coast who, several times each day, took down a beach cobble with a white band ("a wishing stone") from a shelf to teach it to talk. But she views it charitably. "I assume," she writes, "that like any other meaningful effort, the ritual involves sacrifice, the suppression of self-consciousness, and a certain precise tilt of the will, so that the will becomes transparent and hollow, a channel for the work. I wish him well."

Transparent and hollow: a state of mind quite like what's required to find a beach agate, though luck is also involved. Probably that man could have used some luck as well.

My professional opinion is that the mere discovery of a stone gives it voice.

~

Such as that voice is. As Dillard argues, "Nature's silence is its one remark, and every flake of world is a chip off that old mute and immutable block."

Yet the sound of stones being tumbled by the waves is remarkable. It is a thousand knuckles rapping softly at a door.

Monstrous in heavy surf.

"Listen! you hear the grating roar / Of pebbles which the waves draw back, and fling, / At their return, up the high strand, / Begin, and cease, and then again begin . . ."

You can identify beach agates by the innumerable crescents, indentations, on their surfaces, as if imprinted in clay by a fingernail. These are the strike marks they leave on one another.

"Thunder is no longer the voice of an angry god," Carl Jung laments in *Man and His Symbols*, "nor is lightning his avenging missile. No river contains a spirit, no tree is the life principle of a man, no snake the embodiment of wisdom, no mountain cave the home of a great demon. No voices now speak to man from stones, plants, and animals, nor does he speak to them believing they can hear."

Once it was thought that the Thunder Spirits threw agates raucously among the snowy peaks of Mount Hood and Mount Jefferson, where they lived. Now these "thundereggs" are the state rock of Oregon. Their surfaces look pimply, but once cracked, their centers reveal brilliant patterns: star shapes, imagined galaxies. They are mainly found inland, in the sagebrush ocean beyond the Cascades, in rhyolitic lava.

I don't talk to my rocks, but I have sometimes tossed them in my hand or let them rattle musically among the loose change in my pocket.

My back began to ache as I stooped at low tide in the Yachats Bay for more hours than I'd like to admit. My pale neck burned in the sun. It seemed the right price to pay.

Looking for agates, I've found, is as much an exercise of the mind as of the eyes. You must block out most of the world and let in only a particular glint.

By ignoring everything, at least we can see something.

This one is tinted orange and has a ruddy skin-like layer that's almost gone, as if another rub or two of the thumb would separate the stone from its chaff. It is sculpted smooth, but pocked here and there, revealing the mold of the ventricle in which it was formed.

I've learned that the small cavities in the lava of the Oregon coast, those in which agates coalesce, are known as "amygdaloidal," from the Latin for "almond."

Which explains why I have a strange desire to place this stone on my tongue.

"It is believed that to look upon the agate is to rest the eyes," wrote Pliny the Elder. "If held in the mouth, agate quenches the thirst."

Not surprisingly, the amygdalae are those lumps of brain matter, one buried in each hemisphere, responsible for long-term memory consolidation and the sense of smell, among other things. They let us remember the ocean air.

Here's one that reminds me of a lima bean. It's what's known as a "fancy agate," creamy and nontransparent, but laced with a web of orange lines: broken, and then refilled.

The act of collecting is often a psychic pleasure or necessity, but of course it can also be a genuine investment: You can spring for paintings, antiques, cars, and diamonds.

To collect semiprecious fragments would seem an act of protest, then, of withdrawal.

But if collecting springs from a wish to gain control, to possess, then perhaps to gather unique stones is to coerce the earth by holding some of its finest specimens hostage.

Walking below the wrackline in Yachats, I snatched up a perfect, glowing agate. Nearly pellucid, with a hint of green. The size and hue of a peeled grape at Halloween.

But inside drift gauzy clouds.

It is like a glass fishing float washed in from Japan, where they adore the miniature. Where they build pedestals to cradle their "viewing stones," which pose as mountains.

The original crystal ball clearly must have been agate, for it already contains visions within. Rorschachian shapes. Lifelines.

Coincidentally, it's been found that those people who respond unusually to inkblot tests tend to have larger amygdalae, suggesting those regions are central also to creativity.

In agates, people imagine tiny wings. Insects in amber.

When I found that smooth, sea-green stone and turned to show her, a step behind, she gasped, took it into her hands. "It's yours," I said, and immediately I was jealous.

~⌃~

She keeps the agate close to her, now, in the breast pocket of the down jacket she wears as she strides down the brisk avenues of New York City. At night, it hangs in the closet while her heart beats beside me.

I've read somewhere that a person's true appreciation or understanding of a work of art is revealed by how carefully, how purposefully, he holds it.

The heart forms in the cavity of the chest and waits for its collector.

Just north of town, we visited a small cove along a well-traveled beach trail. On a crescent of sand, one family stood by the waves and then raced upslope, laughing, just ahead of the tumbling froth. In the evening light, we found bits of agate even on the pathway, gems stepped on and worn down by passing flip-flops.

One of them, the pebble I now pinch between my thumb and forefinger, is scarlet through and through. A mouse's heart, no larger. It has a network of veins.

Carnelian, I've learned, is a type of orange to fiery red chalcedony. The name suggests "flesh," but the word is actually a sixteenth-century corruption of "cornelian," after the bitter cornel cherry. The stone is supposedly healing, grounding, stimulating. As you might imagine, it's said to enhance blood flow.

I remember the night I found her: It was late, but I could hardly tear my eyes away. We danced together in an old Victorian house, never imagining all these years to come.

Perhaps it was the way we caught the light. What if it had shone differently?

Collecting, I follow my instincts, but I look up, now and then, to take my bearings so as not to overlook any ground: always the worry that the one plot you miss, the one niche you glance at too casually, will inevitably hold the greatest discovery.

Throughout history, agates have been carved into cameos: an oval broach or pendant with a delicate and detailed portrait, often of the beloved in profile. This carving is done at the edge of two layers in an agate so that the background is one color, the relief another.

Large agates are sculpted into cups and figurines, or simply halved to serve as bookends. Others are cut so delicately that they look like a slice of smoked salmon.

In *The Book of Agates*, from which a few items of this collection have been mined, the author and rockhound Lelande Quick understands when he writes, "There are few thrills to equal the satisfaction of personally finding a beautiful agate or other quartz gem and then processing it yourself into a gem of great beauty."

Another memory: Out for agates one morning in Yachats, I spotted a bald eagle on the beach beside a rock. But I suspected it wasn't a rock. Through my binoculars, I watched as the ivory-naped bird picked and tore at the mass with yellow talons as large as my hands. When it flew, I walked across the sand and discovered a headless seal pup. Squatting, I reached out to touch its fur and feel the skin of its flipper. I pinched a claw and its soft sheath slipped off in my grasp. Now it also rests in my bowl.

All these stones, heavy in my hand—somehow, it is they who carry me away. They are an instinctual, if not witless attempt to hold experience by the experience of holding.

Perhaps such a desire is what Emerson means by "Guard well your spare moments."

Or is it simply, as Benjamin writes, the "spring tide of memories which surges toward any collector as he contemplates his possessions"? Those days, just before or after a full moon, when the ocean rises and falls to its extremes, stripping back the sand to awaken gravel beds buried for centuries?

Oh, spare me, you say. But how can I?

There is a fascination that wells up inside me. The Latin *fascinat* means "bewitched." But saying it aloud now, I hear mainly "facet."

As she turned her face in the low western light of a Yachats evening, she looked young and striking. Her skin seemed carnelian in the orange glow across the Pacific, and her laugh crashed over me, as it has so many times. We shared a beer.

But in that moment, I think I also understood that she and I would continue to change at the hands of the carving: the stiff breeze, in good times and in bad, those shifting sands.

"I adore wearing gems," Elizabeth Taylor said, "but not because they are mine. You can't possess radiance, you can only admire it."

Galileo wrote that we covet precious stones because we are afraid: "It is scarcity and plenty that make the vulgar take things to be precious or worthless; they call a diamond very beautiful because it is like pure water, and then would not exchange one for ten barrels of water. Those who so greatly exalt incorruptibility, inalterability, etc. are reduced to talking this way, I believe, by their great desire to go on living, and by the terror they have of death. They do not reflect that if men were immortal, they themselves would never have come into the world."

If I were immortal, oh the collection I would have. Oh the places she and I, we, would go.

~⌄~

Or would it all grow tiresome? As the Chinese proverb goes, "A gem cannot be polished without friction, nor a man perfected without trials."

One might choose to arrange these stones according to chemistry, the way some gather type specimens for a museum drawer. Or one might have an eye only for aesthetics.

A few of the names of agate, its manifold forms: breciatted, ruin, calico, dendritic, ovoid-bearing, faulted, flame, fortification, eye, iris, rainbow, jasp, lace, mocha, moss, plume, sagenitic, stalactitic, tube, landscape.

Those who collect for science often wish to complete their collections, which fulfills a sense of self. It is an accomplishment. But those who collect for the sake of collection, as art, cannot finish for long. Their self will seem to disintegrate.

Many will still believe that collections are a disguise for sheer acquisitiveness, or just misdirected energy. But I hope the activity need not be seen in such a light.

Perhaps that people return to collecting especially in their retirement, when time begins to feel of essence, suggests this gathering is a natural inclination. It triumphs over self-consciousness and often leads to its own discoveries.

"I have been busy with a single art," wrote W. B. Yeats, in preface to one of his collections, "that of the theatre, of a small, unpopular theatre; and this art may well seem to practical men, busy with some programme of industrial or political regeneration, of no more account than the shaping of an agate; and yet in the shaping of an agate, whether in the cutting or the making of the design, one discovers, if one have a speculative mind, thoughts that seem important and principles that may be applied to life itself, and certainly if one does not believe so, one is but a poor cutter of so hard a stone."

I was tempted to write that an agate is like a piece of my own bone, broken off. But it's clear to me, finally, that the closest a body owns to an agate is the eye: Blue or green. Hazelnut and almond.

Not long for its socket.

Even as he went blind, Galileo stared upward at glinting worlds.

Two years after he published his *Natural History*, Pliny the Elder perished in the eruption of Vesuvius that buried Pompeii in 79 A.D., a pyroclastic flow that rolled over the countryside, creating new hollows in layers of ash.

Hollows in which agates may well form, when we are all gone and yet another epoch has descended upon the earth.

Agates in the shapes of bodies, clinging to one another.

The Afterlife

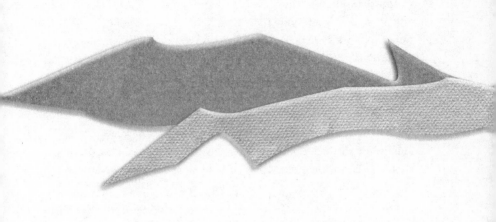

A salmon's second journey begins with its "collection." At the Cole M. Rivers Hatchery north of Medford, Oregon, the crowder is drawn through the holding pond once a week, May through August, pushing the fish toward the rear, toward the spawning house. When I visited one June, three hundred spring Chinook were loitering, miraculously returned from the ocean to the place where, for them, it had all begun. They were conceived artificially and released as fingerling smolt into the Rogue River, which ushered them through Shady Cove and Grants Pass—all the way to Gold Beach and the Pacific. A fraction of them reach the ocean. A fraction of those return. These were the prodigal .003 percent, each fifteen or twenty pounds of sauntering muscle wrapped in silver.

Cole Rivers is an industrial-strength facility, a real doozy. "No one wants to work here," David Pease, the assistant manager, said with a measure of pride. Tall and laid-back, with curly brown hair, Dave was in a short-sleeved beige Oregon Department of Fish and Wildlife uniform and khaki shorts, a classic game-warden look. There are eighty-seven ponds on the Cole Rivers campus, while the typical Oregon hatchery has about fifteen. On the other hand, elsewhere employees must wade through ponds with screens during the dead, or drizzle, of winter to corral their fish. Here you have the crowder, which is much like the automatic sweeper on a bowling lane.

But it can't handle three hundred Chinook. Not close. Most, in fact, weigh more than your average bowling ball, and the contraption began to moan and screech as it approached the spawning house. The operator, Ada Carnes, a hatchery technician with long blond hair, freckles, and deep-set eyes, backed off and lifted the gate of the crowder a touch, letting some fish escape underneath. A reprieve. Instantly they darted the length of the pen, sleek torpedoes with jaws, speckled and scarred. Many had visible hook wounds on their flanks, pink gashes. Some were "whiteheads," covered with a fungus where they had scraped the protective mucus from their scales while forging upriver, over rock. "They're dying," Dave said. All of them.

Salmon stop eating when they enter freshwater. Their whole purpose, then, is to flash upstream, and their intestines shrivel inside their massive bodies to make room for swelling gonads. The feast is over; the ocean becomes a memory. As they push on, they lean on their reserves. Become lean. By the time they reach their natal waters, salmon give "running on empty" new meaning. The jaws of the male elongate and hook, becoming a "kype" that broadcasts his prowess. A female excavates a redd in gravel with her tail and deposits her eggs, which, at that same moment, are met by a cloud of milt, his offering, a cloud settling and dissipating in a blink of current. She guards her brood until she has no strength. Then her body releases to the current and drifts, already disintegrating, to an eddy or shoulder of mud where its essentials are reabsorbed: by crawdads; by raccoons, bears, and bald eagles; by trees even several hundred feet from the bank; and by salmon fry, those thousands of unknowing mouths that need every advantage if they're to swim the Rogue and home again, to die.

The water began to boil. As the crowder neared the back wall, the hulking fish panicked and frenzied in the diminished space, throwing their fins into the air. A salmon's world, of course, is immeasurable: the ocean, the wild length of the Rogue, 157 miles of rapids and anglers to the hatchery. Raked together in this concrete pool, perhaps these salmon sensed time was finally closing in. That something was lifting them. The crowder has a bottom shelf, and once the school was pinned, their floor rose—Ada elevated it—until they piled at the surface and about fifteen spilled through a gap and down a wide ramp into the facility. To the "brail" that would subdue them with an electric pulse.

Momentarily. "If you don't quiet them," said Dave, "they beat you up. They'll put a hurting on you." Ada raised the brail ten feet and tilted it so the fish would pour onto the sorting table. The salmon flopped despite the current that had just coursed through their blood-orange interiors. But, not as much. Their heavy domes and tails thumped on the stainless steel, but they weren't "hot," as Dave called it. Another technician wearing a Stetson and camouflage hip-waders grasped each Chinook and stilled it, best he could, with one hand over its golden eye and the other on its tail. He slid each to Ada. Both of them wore non-abrasive cotton gloves that quickly became covered in slime.

It was an inspection line of two. The hatchery's first need is brood-stock—fish to spawn next year's smolts—and throughout the four-month season, Dave and company select a variety of sizes to keep the gene pool diverse. Each week, they sort the arrivals and fill quotas along the spectrum. In front of the technicians were six chutes, dark tunnels, each a vacuum leading to a different outdoor pond: something like the pneumatic tubes that propelled canisters to the tellers at drive-through banks of old. Ada passed each fish, briefly, into a metal detector, and pulled them out by the tail. If the buzzer sounded, she dropped the fish headfirst into Chute 2, no questions asked. As a smolt, it had been implanted with a tiny coded-wire tag (in the nasal cartilage of its snout), which would be reclaimed to see when and where it had been reared. If there was no alarm, then Ada measured the fish and called out its sex and length in millimeters. Dave would glance at his data sheet, holler over the sound of water, and scratch tallies:

"Buck 670," yelled Ada.

"Yeah," shouted Dave.

"Buck 800."

"Yeah."

"Buck 870."

That's thirty-four inches.

"No."

"Oh, whoops, got him anyway . . . How about hen 810?"

"Yeah."

"Hen 830."

"Yeah," said Dave, as a three-inch insect called a salmon fly, hatched out of the river with orange legs and abdomen, alighted on the small desk where he sat perched on a stool.

"Buck 800."

"Yeah."

"Buck 830."

"No."

"This one's comical," said Ada's cowboy partner, as he passed her the next.

"How about a buck sub-350?" she said.

"Sure," Dave replied. The smallest are known as "jacks," males that try to spawn after a single year in the ocean. Fewer than ten pounds, and sneaky.

The sorting occurs in episodes of only a few minutes, fifteen or twenty fish at a time so they aren't out of water too long. Then the crowder lifts again and more cascade onto the brail—*zap*. Over the course of the morning, Dave shouted "No" more often as broodstock requirements were filled. He referred to his paper, and each decision was impersonal. Nonetheless, it reminded me of an emperor lifting his thumb up, or down. "Yeah" sends the salmon into Chute 4 (after it receives an injection, to prevent disease) for breeding in the fall. Those genes, randomly selected, will carry on—have a chance to—and four years later (jacks aside), a fraction of the resulting smolt will return transformed. But a "No" from Dave sends the salmon hurtling through the black hole of Chute 6, for a moment, and into the pond reserved for "excess." The afterlife begins.

You can't quite see it from the hatchery, but the dam is there, lurking around the bend. Cole Rivers was built by the Army Corps of Engineers in 1973 in the wake, quite literally, of Lost Creek Lake, a reservoir created for flood control. The earthen wall is three hundred feet tall, three thousand long. More than six hundred square miles of mountain drain to the reservoir, and the dam spoiled all those spawning grounds: the upper Rogue and its headwaters. In essence, the fifty-eight-acre hatchery, with the help of sixteen employees and sophisticated fishery science, is to stand for those hundreds of miles of intricate streambed, those sinuous bends and side creeks filled with snags, plunges, and crystalline gravel stretches.

But what becomes of the thousands of grown salmon that, each year, are savvy or lucky enough to avoid a hook on their way home and yet aren't selected for breeding? Once broodstock is in hand, the hatchery has no need for them, those colossal extra. In the parlance of ODFW, they must be "disposed" of, and a hierarchy, a ladder, exists for their "disposition." Though the natural abundance of wild salmon in the Northwest is largely gone—70 percent of Oregon's salmon are from hatcheries—even in death, these steel-tank-raised brethren continue to migrate toward hopeful ends.

About four thousand early birds at Cole Rivers are "recycled": A few hundred salmon at a time are driven downstream in a tanker truck and, in the town of Gold Hill, poured back into the Rogue. Recycling capitalizes on the fishes' proven fitness to offer anglers a chance at redemption. Slightly fewer than half of recycled fish successfully run the gauntlet again and climb back into the hatchery. But some of them swim the thirty-six miles in less than twelve days. That's hauling. Pre-release, the hatchery hole-punches their gill plates so that they won't be counted twice in the run total.

Another tributary is "stream enrichment." Since wild populations have dwindled, far fewer salmon now decay in rivers and creeks, and the ecosystem suffers. As they melt into the shallows, salmon leave an important wave of nourishment from the ocean. Now ODFW casts carcasses into waterways, trying to replicate the fertile casualties of former times. They've used helicopters—very messy. Pitchforking them from bridges is cheaper, with the added advantage that it's still good and messy. Personally enriching for volunteers.

Fish are also sold commercially to American Canadian Fisheries, a company in Washington State that sells fillets to stores like Safeway. You could be eating a marinated Cole Rivers fish tonight for dinner. The Rogue's salmon are often a sore sight when they arrive at the hatchery. "But if you cut them open," Dave Pease told me, "they're an awesome-looking fish. I mean it's red, bright red." Hatchery programs are supported by this "carcass fund."

Later in the season, American Canadian Fisheries then donates its services, filleting and packaging salmon for the Oregon Food Bank, which sends the fish throughout the state to outlets like the St. Henry's Food Pantry in Gresham, near Portland. Its manager, Ann Prester, told me that in recent Februaries they've given coho, a winter arrival, to everyone who walks through their door: thirty-five families a day, almost four hundred pounds of salmon a year. "These are people who don't have access to salmon otherwise, not at eight to nine dollars a pound," said Ann. "Their eyes just light up." Many have never seen a living salmon, she said, but they're thankful it doesn't live in a can.

Before all these possible ends for excess salmon, however, Oregon tribes are allowed fish for ceremony and subsistence, as outlined in their treaties. I had journeyed to the Rogue to see salmon be given to the Cow Creek Band of Umpqua Tribe of Indians. This was the tributary of a salmon's disposition I hoped to follow to its terminus. Members of the Cow Creek Band would arrive in the morning to haul off a fresh load for their annual powwow and salmon rite in a couple of weeks. I asked Dave when the fish I'd just seen collected would go to the chair. To the brail, for a stronger pulse. "If you come back around nine, you should be fine," he said.

⌒‿⌒

I camped on the Rogue's upper reaches that night, above what's known as Natural Bridge, where the stream is swallowed by a lava tube and disappears briefly from the light, a molten river turned cold. Down unmarked jeep trails, I found a stretch that poured over the wall of a deep basalt channel within the river, creating a long curtain of white facing the bank. In the morning, I rolled up my sleeping bag and drove the twenty minutes through towering pines to Lost Creek Lake, where the river also disappears.

To my chagrin, the fish had been zapped ahead of schedule. The Cow Creek Band's volunteers were backing up a trailer on which rested two identical, empty turquoise containers, perhaps five hundred gallons each. I met Teri Hansen, her son Jake Ansures, and his five-year-old boy as they stepped from their white pickup. She had satiny black hair to her waist, bangs cascading down her brow, and a powwow T-shirt with short red sleeves that exposed her pale arms. Her voice was smoky, graveled. She was a clerk for the tribal court. Jake was athletic, in a scarlet DC skater's shirt and a black cap with a stiff brim. His eyes were wide, his grin elastic. He worked as a sales and marketing manager for the tribe-owned Umpqua Indian Foods, known for its steak jerky.

Dave soon drove out of the spawning house on a forklift with a white plastic container that looked like a giant mail bin, a USPS flat tub. Inside was a thousand pounds of salmon. Fifty-nine fish, as it turned out. Their skins were mottled, jaundiced in patches. Some were without their snouts, which had been removed—severed—to extract those coded-wire tags. Other tribes want all of their fish entire, but the Cow Creek Band needed only two. "You could gut and fillet them also, if you'd like," said Teri. Dave laughed, said his crew probably wouldn't go for that.

The lift whined as Dave tilted the bin, and another technician swept and dragged the fish so that they spilled, slowly, into the tribe's turquoise counterpart, leaving it speckled and streaked with drip marks. In black gloves and a white apron, he had the appearance of a butcher, and he took his time, to minimize splatters. He'd done this before. Blood as thick as syrup ran over the sides and, when I edged a little too close, my shirt paid a small price. My forearm, too. Jake shoveled ice into the fish as they fell like a lumbering waterfall, and before long it seemed they would all fit in just one of the turquoise containers. "One less tote to clean," said Dave.

When the fish were tied down, we took a quick stroll around the grounds. The ponds looked like lap pools, but were tented with netting to prevent gulls and eagles, and maybe anglers, from diving in. They rippled with the backs of trout and salmon, and juveniles at all stages: fry, parr, smolt. We walked toward the fish ladder and collection pond. Sun poured through the ladder's entrance, a roofless hallway into the river, where big fish were holding in the shadow of the wall. You could see them if you trained your eyes, if you squinted, and if the school nosed momentarily into the slant of light. They were poised as if waiting for some signal. Some decision.

I asked Jake when he had caught his first salmon. Nine or ten, he said. I asked after its size. "It was all right," he said. "It tasted good, I can tell you that much."

He put his kid on his shoulders, and they stood on the bridge above the ladder's last step, the one that ultimately lofted those scarred-backs from the Rogue to their origin. Through the grate that separated the pen from the ladder, water roiled in an incandescent foam. As we stared down, mesmerized, instantly and inexplicably a slick teardrop form broke the surface and glided through the air into the hatchery's motionless pool. "Ooooh," we all said, as the salmon hurdled.

"Good job," said Teri. "He wasn't wasting any time."

"He looked like he knew what he was doing," said Jake.

Then another he, or she, leaped up and deflected off the concrete sidewall into the holding pond. It was a triumph and a bittersweet moment of finality. For this was the gate to heaven. And these fish were a day late for the ceremony.

The totes pulled out of the hatchery lot, and I followed. Salmon flies fluttered before the windshield and lay dead on the pavement. We turned toward Medford, but before we'd gone far, the fish swung right and headed skyward. *Caution*, a road sign announced, *Limited*

Maintenance After Dark. This was OR-227, Tiller Trail Highway, the short-but-steep cut to Canyonville over a mountain pass. We were lifting the fish from their native drainage to the neighboring one, the South Umpqua, which seemed to embody the peculiar migrations of the modern age: Even in death, these fish were being transplanted to another river, the way planes let trout free-fall into alpine lakes; the way seedling invasive mussels hitch rides on trailered hulls.

The road was hemmed in with fir, oak, and lustrous madrone. Then it ran through clear-cuts with heaping slash piles hard on the shoulder. I felt as if I were in the wake of something remarkable, clandestine even. The turquoise of the container took on a kind of glow, freighted not just with the weight of the fish, but with their import to the tribe and the Northwest more broadly. The drive was a procession, a caravan into the clouds.

We crested the ridge and slalomed to Elk Creek, which joined the South Umpqua River at the townlet of Tiller, where many of the Cow Creek's forbears are buried. They had built the first roads and bridges in the drainage for the government, some over the mountains on old Indian trails. Teri and her boys stopped at the general store. Inside was a framed black-and-white photo of a man with a pistol in one hand and a skunk dangling by its tail in the other: He was an official Douglas County champion skunk hunter, a dubious accolade. Teri and her grandson bought morning ice cream bars. Then we flowed on, past sturdy and decrepit barns, stacked wagon wheels, and shrink-wrapped hay bales that looked like fresh mozzarella in the fields; past signs for *Eggs $2* (then, closer to Canyonville, *Eggs $3*) and *Creation Camp*.

Finally we reached the river's confluence with I-5 and the Seven Feathers Casino, the Cow Creek's cash cow. What had started, in 1992, as a bingo parlor had become a three-hundred-room resort with a thousand slot machines on its main floor. Not too big, as casinos go. Seven feathers, of course, is symbolic: The tribe, as reconstituted, began with just seven families, the survivors of the Rogue Indian Wars of 1855–1856. They had hidden from vigilante settlers in the mountains east of Tiller. Thus the tribe's emblem is of seven feathers tied to a single staff, a common destiny. But there is other iconography. In front of the hotel's porte cochere stands a heroic statue with its wings swept upward, its talons outstretched: It's the largest bronze eagle in the world, at thirty-three feet tall and ten thousand pounds, and it's striking a salmon.

The turquoise totes snaked to the rear of the casino and backed into an open bay lined with shelves of humongous cans and twenty-five-pound bags of flour and sugar that were heavier, just barely, than the salmon. I parked and was escorted down a corridor to obtain a behind-the-scenes badge that read *Visitor*. When I returned, the dead had been unloaded in clear plastic tubs and carted into the commercial kitchen, where a dozen chefs awaited, all in white. They had donned a hierarchy of toques and berets, and on the stainless steel preparation tables before them, each had a V-shaped wooden carving board to cradle a fish. The casino had made these some years earlier for precisely this purpose, the annual pre-powwow cleaning. It was clear much bleach would be needed.

Several other tribal members arrived to help prepare the salmon, including Kelly Rondeau. He wore a faded T-shirt printed with a wrap-around American flag and sunglasses atop his ashen hair tied in a pony-tail. His face was tall, his nose broad and prominent, his rugged smile lines framed by a moustache. "So which one do I get to take home?" he said jokingly. Half-jokingly. The Rondeau family is one of the seven original. His grandfather had been instrumental in starting the casino, and now Kelly was on the tribal board. He told me of the 180,000 steel-head smolt the tribe had helped release into the South Umpqua over the last decade. "We're going to have to start claiming some of them," he said, wryly.

I spent time with Dennis, *Buffet Captain*, and Victoria, *Sports Bar Cook*. Dennis did the cutting. With a forceful cleave behind the gills, their heads, those sunken and rosy eyes, were the first to go. For those that had already lost their snouts, it seemed an act of mercy, aesthetic at least. In many of the salmon, this first cut revealed shining clusters of roe behind the shoulders: translucent orange orbs that, in another life, would have overwintered in the small crater of a redd to first become big-eyed alevin, which stay hidden under gravel with a yolk sack slung to their bellies. The chefs scooped these refulgent masses into gallon bags for those on hand and lucky elders. Kelly held up two bags as if raising the spoils of a contest. He would thread them like beads onto a hook and bait steelhead, but one could also flash-fry them with flour.

The fish were butterflied, from the anal duct upward. The glossy innards were slung into trash cans. With the knife's tip—or better, a fingernail—the chefs scraped out the coagulated red that ran against those spines newly exposed to the fluorescent light. I asked Vicky what this spinal gunk was called. "Spinal gunk," she answered with her signature staccato laugh. "I have no idea." I've since learned that it's called the bloodline: the river within the fish, those arteries and veins that allow these dense muscles to thrust and quiver, and fight their way home.

"I like fish," said Vicky, "but not in the raw. Don't think I'd want to do this for a living." She did the washing in a stainless basin, her chubby hands swirling inside the open book of each salmon. "This is not how they get'm at Safeway," she added. The steady sound of the faucets was like a recollection of a river and, rinsed, the salmon recovered some of their silver brilliance. They'd given up their heads, but not their tails; not their elegance. Teri, Kelly, and the other members of the tribe helped package them: shrouded in plastic garbage bags, wrapped in white butcher paper, stacked once more on a stainless cart. Some were marked with a Sharpie for the mid-July powwow, others were reserved for a second event. Teri selected a small fish, one to fit her oven. "Everything you do, you do with a prayer and good thoughts," she said. ("What is that," asked Kelly, "a trout?") The rest were wheeled into the freezer.

Two weeks later, I found myself on the Rogue-Umpqua Divide, staring out from under a fleece cap at a vast series of drainages. The Cascades' ridges seemed to live up to the range's name: a long line of waves being pulled down, slowly, by gravity. The snow had just melted, the earth was soupy, and the mosquitoes whined. I immediately had to stoke a fire to ward off these evil spirits. But there were tiny yellow violets strewn across the wet jeep tracks, and I was otherwise alone. At dusk, I became apprehensive for a moment, thinking a truck was coming around the bend. But it was the moon.

In summer, the Cow Creek Band also climbed to these heights, which were known, almost mythically, as the Huckleberry Patch, as if it were the first and only berry-picking spot on earth. They felt closer to the Great Spirit at these heights, slept in the open air, and dried venison and berries for winter. Sometimes they descended to the Rogue to hunt and trade, and went across Natural Bridge as far as the Klamath Marsh. They roamed west into the Coast Range or through the Rogue watershed to the Siskiyous. They told origin stories about the cradle of Crater Lake, Mount Mazama, whose shield feeds the Rogue and so, with a little help from the government, gave life to the salmon frozen in Canyonville. Here on the divide, the idea of carrying fish between drainages suddenly didn't seem so unnatural: From this edge, water ran two ways, arbitrarily, and as a result entered the sea one hundred miles apart. But this view described the Cow Creek's territory long before it was renamed a "wilderness" even as surrounding hillsides began to lose their trees.

In 1853, the Cow Creeks became the second tribe in Oregon to forge a treaty with the United States, ceding more than eight hundred square miles of land in the South Umpqua watershed, though they had no idea something so essential could be signed away. They were compensated 2.3 cents per acre, and the United States turned around and sold those acres to settlers for a dollar and a quarter. Afterward, the Cow Creeks were literally and figuratively driven into the hills, toward the Rogue-Umpqua Divide. Though they were promised a reservation and more, the tribe was only truly recognized when, without notice, its sovereignty was dismissed by the Western Oregon Indian Termination Act of 1954. But in 1982, Congress reacknowledged the tribe and, two years later, the courts awarded it 1.5 million dollars for lands lost. The tribe's leaders prudently rolled the sum into a trust that helped spawn the casino and, now, a growing empire in Douglas County.

Come morning, I drove in low gear down the swelling Umpqua, to the falls where the Cow Creek Band had long congregated for salmon and still gathered for its summer powwow. The campground was a clearing nestled against a ridge on the north side of the river, an old Forest Service camp ideal for large groups. Tribal members had arrived the night before and parked among the trees at the meadow's edge, in the sanity of the shade, in their annual spots. Families stretched tarps between RVs and firs to bridge their camps and shelter their stoves. The two teepees present were vastly outnumbered and looked out of place (historic Cow Creek houses were dugouts with pine-board ceilings). Space was already tight, so I pitched my tent in the meadow, in the morning shadow of a lone oak tree, poison oak ascending its trunk. I should have thought about how that might make me stand out a little, but no one cared. The tribe welcomed me. When my unstaked tent blew off that afternoon, someone corralled it and tied it to my roof rack like a balloon.

Before noon, an assembly line began to gather around a long, pine-green folding table, and there I reconnected with Teri and Kelly. Supplies were waiting: cylindrical cartons of Morton salt, fresh-cut lemon wheels in gallon Ziplocs, terrifying jars of minced garlic, and most important, an unopened case of mayonnaise. All to dress the fish. Also a box of sweet Walla Walla onions, which first had to be chopped. It was a merry affair with few tears. "Look at all these Indians, with all these knives," said Kelly, "and everyone's still got their hair."

Then at the head of the table stood a man named Wade Wells, bare- and barrel-chested, in sunglasses, his slate hair crew cut. He lived in Sutherlin, just north of Roseburg, and coached sports at the high school from which he graduated; his upper arms were about as swole as the fish. He kicked off the proceedings by pulling a loud, blinding sheet of tinfoil over his head so that it illuminated, then shaded, his torso, and he brought it forward through the breeze, a metallic cape trailing behind him. "Dancing with foil," shouted one onlooker. It stretched clear across the table.

Two young men with a Marine disposition were assigned to unwrapping the thawed fish from their garbage bags and carrying them by their tails (gingerly, firmly) to the foil. The fish were headless and, with scissors, the guys now docked the stiff points of their tails so they wouldn't tear the foil. As each fish was laid down on a new sheet of foil, Kelly massaged its flesh with mayo, inside and out, his disposable gloves nearly hidden in a swirl of egg yolk and vinegar. "Caress that fish," said a woman named Jessica Jackson, an Air Force member in a maroon tank top and short brown braids. "Let the fish know it's loved." At some point during the assembly, Kelly held up his hands, grinned, and said, "All I have to do is clap my hands and everyone gets mayonnaised."

Others hovered over each fish momentarily to shake on more salt than you would believe and stuff it with handfuls of yellow garlic and chopped onions, a surrogate for the innards removed in the casino weeks ago. Then the "lemon girl" took her turn and placed four or five slices inside each belly, all in a neat, overlapping row. Trying to clamp the cavity shut was like wrestling a suitcase. Finally, Jessica and the day's chef, Barry McKown, each lifted one side of the foil, creating a tall aluminum A-frame. They rolled the sheet's ends together until the fish was snug. They folded and crimped the long edges to finish the pocket. Then Wade tore more foil, and each fish was double-wrapped. "Got'a keep my juice," Barry reminded us. "Double-wrapping helps me out a lot."

"We are a well-oiled machine!" Jessica declared, which was not untrue. Especially considering the mayo. She had the flare and spunk of a leader. Wade began to sing—*Ain't no sunshine when she's gone—Got'a whole lotta of love*—as he drew out long crackling sheets, one after the next, and danced them forward. The foil caught the sun through the cumulus and reflected it onto the faces of the volunteers. It was like a photo shoot. "Mayo, Led Zeppelin, shiny lights—I was starting to have a little seizure," said Wade. Again the salmon piled up, this time like silver ingots, until there were eighteen. Each lay wrapped as if in homage to its gleaming self, only, in this life, with straight edges.

Finally, the ceremonial fish: cleaned, but otherwise untouched. Still with its head and tail. This one was sacred, the core of the afternoon. This particular Chinook, of the thousands that would return to the Cole Rivers Hatchery. "We only got two of them," said Jessica, urging caution. "Can't be running to the store to get another one." In case of disaster, a second entire fish was on hand, still with its head, but it was slated for a fall powwow. The tribe had grown so large—to more than sixteen hundred members—that now it hosted two intertribal gatherings each year.

The guys brought the fish before us. Its face, its robust lower jaw, was bruised and rubicund, as if the blood were welling back after the long cold spell of the casino. Its bronze eye was sunken slightly, but still bright: That you could meet the gaze of this fish did seem important; you knew whom you were bound to. We all looked into its pupil, which had seen something of the Pacific's depth and returned to stare blankly at us.

The men held the heavy animal so that it could be blessed by Grandma Gin. She was indeed warm and grandmotherly, with deep laugh lines and eye shadow. Her bangs were coiffed, but her dyed auburn hair was otherwise long and straight down her shoulders and back. She intently wound a smudge stick—a smoldering bundle of white sage—around the fish's body, leaving a trail of incense that carried me to the dry side of the Cascades, to the brush of the high steppe. To rain shadow. She trailed it over the pile of aluminum packets, and around each volunteer, her lips moving as she went. Once finished, she replaced the lit smudge in the warty trough of an opalescent abalone shell. The smoke would allow only good spirits.

The fish was laid on the foil and slathered in sacred mayo. Then the matron of the tribe, the eldest elder, was brought forward by Grandma Gin to formally bless the fish, as was tradition. "Okay, Kelly," said Grandma Gin, "you want to come stand near Aunt Rena? She's going to say her prayer." Rena was slightly hunched and held to a smooth walking stick. She peered out from thin-rimmed tortoise-shell spectacles and pursed her small mouth. Her white hair was short, hardly longer than the lobes of her ears. She wore a pink windbreaker and a hat that said *Native Pride*. This year was Rena's first as eldest, and she was trembling with emotion. She was ninety-four years old.

"Come on, my powwow princess," said Gin, "you can do it. We love you."

Rena sobbed and her words were a quiet babble into Gin's ear.

"I know you do," said Gin. "But he is here, in his spirit. All our ancestors are here in their spirit."

Aunt Rena had lost her husband decades ago, but he was in mind, very much so. They were married before she finished high school (she'd started school late, at the age of nine). He had worked for the New Deal's Civilian Conservation Corps before they moved to Union, on the dry side of the Cascades, for his job with the railroad.

"All right, Grandfather," said Rena, finding strength. "I ask that you bless the people that gave us the fish. And I ask you to bless each and everyone that wrapped it . . . Thank you, God, for giving us the fish that we will partake of our elders with. That's all."

"Aho," said the crowd. "Aho."

Gin rubbed Rena's shoulder. "There you go," she said. "He's here. He's here. Come on."

"God bless you, Aunt Rena," said Kelly. "My dad's here, too."

"The brightest star in the sky last night was Buster," Rena replied, referring to Kelly's father. The Cow Creeks also believe that a shooting star is a spirit arriving to inhabit a newborn.

"Yeah, I know," said Kelly. "That's what I was thinking."

"They're all here, honey," said Gin. "An eagle flew over this morning, remember, Kelly? When we raised the flag, the eagle went over."

"He did?" said Rena.

"Yes, he did," said Gin. "Your eagle . . . he's here. He's teasing you . . ."

"He didn't come and bow to me, that rascal."

"He will," said Kelly.

"You'll see him," said Gin.

Boys had been up all night tending the pit. It had been dug in the meadow, not far from the logs, those whole trees that framed the dancing grounds, where men in full regalia would circle and stomp during Grand Entry on Saturday. Cedar billets had been thrown down and kindled, and the kids had stoked the fire through the dawn to build up coals. One boy was discovered asleep on the dirt pile from the pit's excavation. Wade had kicked his foot away from the flaming wood (his buddies had made no motion to help). In midafternoon, the boys still hadn't retired to their sleeping bags; in the shade, with a subwoofer, they were having a deliriously good time as local heroes.

Traditionally, salmon fillets were splayed across western redcedar staves and leaned over a fire. The cedar's natural oils flavored the fish, while its tannins resisted flame. Now, however, a giant grate with legs had been pulled over the coals, a devilish cot, and Barry McKown laid the fish on it in two shining rows. Nineteen fish shoulder to shoulder, the way they might jostle upstream through a gauntlet, but here insulated on a pyre. I'd met Barry first in the casino kitchen. As powwow grill master, he had come for a glimpse of this year's raw material, which met his approval. He'd worn a Hawaiian shirt then, and he wore another one now, white palm fronds on blue. Barry has a round face and mustache, and his brown locks stayed stuffed under a Cow Creek cap with an embroidered bald eagle hauling off a salmon. Of course.

Barry had been in charge as chef for twenty-six years. It was Kelly's grandfather who had asked him if he would take over the cooking duty. "Yeaaaaaah," Barry had replied, in his rural-dude twang. "It would be a great honor." Each year since, he has baked roughly three hundred pounds of Chinook, about twenty fish. He flips them every half hour, for three and a half hours. Afterward he would "stack them like wood" under a tarp. "As it's cooling down," said Barry, "it sucks that juice back in." His priority was wholeheartedly "my juices" and "extra juicy."

If to chop your own wood is to warm yourself twice, then Barry was satisfying his hunger seven times over—and warming himself, too, because this sucker was hot. In preparation for a flip, he donned heavy leather gloves that covered his wrists and forearms, just like those the woman from Wildlife Images wore as she handled the captive bald eagle (or the barn owl, or the Swainson's hawk) at the powwow for show-and-tell. But as Barry cradled the heavy fish and set them back down—rotating them from the grill's interior to its periphery—it was more like placing sandbags during a flood. This year, he was shielding his bare shins with a sheet of corrugated tin. "I've been burning my feet and legs," he said. "Only took me twenty-six years to figure that out." With each flip, sweat appeared instantly on his brow and streamed down his cheeks.

A wall clock was leaned against a fir beside Barry's camping chair to help him monitor the fishes' progress. He grew slightly concerned. The salmon were taking awful long to bake and time was beginning to run short, the shadows lengthening across the parched meadow. He didn't have his briquettes, as he was supposed to—the organizing committee had forgotten them—and the cedar wasn't white-hot. "I could get scalped and hung up from a tree if the fish don't come out," Barry said. As he handled the fish, gradually they reclaimed their native shape, the foil conforming to their curved bodies, while leaking juice browned their crinkled topography and sizzled away. Across one end of the grate, roasted lemon rings lay scattered like a spill of enormous roe.

Another flip, and then Barry took me to the river. In a year of heavy snows, the South Umpqua Falls plunges classically along the north bank, the near side: headlong from ledges, in a torrent. But on the far side, it's less a falls than a glide. A smooth, low dome of bedrock spreads the water so thin that it appears as a ten-thousand-thread sheet pulled across the stone. People were walking up and down this easy cascade barefoot or in flip-flops. A woman held the hands of her two kids, one a toddler, as they made the brilliant, flowing descent in yellow and red life jackets.

In the old days, salmon also walked up the dome with their bellies on the slab and their dorsa in the air—and they still made the climb, apparently, on certain moonlit nights. Once the tribe built weirs atop the falls and set cone-shaped traps, woven of hazel shoots, in the fast channels below, so that the thwarted fish would be swept back into these basket funnels and pinned by the strong current. You're no longer allowed to fish for salmon at the falls, but sometimes, Teri had told me earlier, you can glimpse them deep in the pool, if you swim with a mask. If you brave the cold. "But you seldom see them," said Barry, "there are so many people here making noise."

Kids were hollering and sliding off the ledge into the bracing pool. Some on inner tubes, others on their bums. The seasoned or foolhardy launched into backflips. "Yeah, it's really high," said Barry. "Big falls this year. Beautiful. I love the way the water just rolls down the hump of rock." It was six or seven inches above usual, he estimated. A concrete fish ladder ran up the north bank for times of low water, when the dome might go dry. "Might as well make it easy on them," said Barry. The ladder was like the one at Cole Rivers, only smaller, and these stairs led to a different kind of afterlife. The ascending fish would forge into the narrowing mountains, toward the Rogue-Umpqua Divide, to offer their offspring the best possible start: cold, clear water.

"This place can fill with hundreds of people," said Barry, as he surveyed the bright, roaring scene and looked at his watch. The salmon were waiting. Barry had started coming to the powwow in his midtwenties, and this year was his thirty-seventh. "All the people that had to work today," he said, "they're going to come in this weekend. They're going to start coming in bumper-to-bumper." They would be hungry.

Jessica wasn't happy about the state of the sacred fish. It wasn't exactly cooked, and tension was simmering between her and Barry. Traditionally, the meat of the one ceremonial salmon is gleaned and eaten, while the skin and bones are left untouched. Jessica and a friend named Lottie were hunched over the table like surgeons over a patient, and this procedure wasn't going well. Normally the skin peels back easily, as one, but this time it was resisting—and then tearing. Inside, the fillet was sloppy, a vibrant raw orange, as wet as a kiss. Slipping the flesh from the hair-thin bones was nearly impossible.

Between subtle frowns, Jessica told me the origin of the tribe's reverence for salmon, a story that, in its essence, holds true for much of the Native culture of Cascadia: "Long ago, animals walked upright like humans. Once we arrived, some of the animals realized we were starving. We weren't able to feed ourselves. Salmon was one of those animals, and they said, 'We will provide for you and be your food.' So that's when they went to the river and became fish. They go out to sea, they come back, and the females of course give birth, but their body nourishes their fry. That's why we honor them. The salmon is one of those people that stepped forward. They chose to give their life up for us, so that we wouldn't starve." Implicit in this story, of course, is that we are the "fry" of salmon, that they are our parents even as we catch and devour them—as perhaps all children do—and sometimes make an awful mess of them, as we have with dams and stream degradation in more recent history.

The ceremonial salmon was in tatters. When Jessica and Lottie were finished, they endeavored, carefully, to reconstruct the fish. But frankly, it looked monstrous as it lay on the tray, with its shredded gray skin draped unconvincingly across its midsection like a blanket full of holes. Its eyes had baked to an opaque white. The conspicuous teeth of its upper jaw suggested a mischievous smirk, as if the salmon knew of and enjoyed the trouble it had made. It was sprawled in a slurry of mayo, fat, and sloppy orange shards.

"Turned out nice, didn't it?" Barry said.

"No," said Jessica.

"Yeah, it's not done yet," Barry replied. "The fire never was hot. I didn't have my briquettes here this year. They just lowered the grate, instead."

Aunt Rena noticed when she was led forward for another blessing.

"It's not cooking fast enough, so this is what they did," said Grandma Gin. "Will that be okay?"

We held our breath.

"That'll be all right," Aunt Rena said, to palpable exhales. "We will have it this way, this year. But next year, it *better* be done. They better put it on earlier than you did today."

"Give me briquettes next year, and it'll be done," Barry said softly.

The boys lined up in front of the table, three still in their baby fat, two others older and slimming. Their T-shirts told of the region and its predilections: *Go Ducks* with the bright yellow O of the university in Eugene; skater designs with frenetic lettering and skulls wearing bejeweled crowns; the 18th Annual Strawberry Cup at the Willamette Speedway in Lebanon, Oregon (sponsored by Napa Auto Parts). One boy sported a fauxhawk, his hair shaved on each side, but robust, tussled, on top. Another had an epic scrape across his cheek, a raspberry from an encounter with pavement. A third was much taller than the rest. Somehow he'd evaded this rite of passage, until now.

The kids didn't look so much Native, as American, both healthy and unkempt. They looked as if they'd been camping in the woods of Oregon. The five of them stood before tribal elder Robert Van-Norman, a retired logger and Vietnam vet, who held the wing of an eagle and slowly fanned the smudge smoldering in its abalone. The white tendrils drifted over the boys, and over the fish presented on a tray lined, naturally, with foil. It remained a horrendous sight, which made it the more serious and captivating. Behind the kids stood friends and family, and the dedicated few—not the whole tribe—some leaning against a faded pickup with peeling blue paint. This included girls in the shortest of jean shorts, generous belt buckles, and blond pigtails, and I wondered what they made of this moment: whether they felt brave and left out.

Aunt Rena again:

"Grandfather, I would like for you to bless us . . . and the river, who has provided us with the salmon that we will partake of at the elder's dinner. That's all I've got to say."

"Aho," the crowd echoed. "Aho."

"Now those boys are going to go down in a minute," Rena continued, turning to address them. "When you get ready to push this fish in the river, you pick up that foil and slide it right to the bottom. Robert, you get busy when they start that into the water. You say a prayer. All right, that's it, honey.

"I don't know whether I did it right," Aunt Rena said to Grandma Gin.

"You did it right," she replied.

"We can do it our way," said Kelly.

Robert then took over as master of ceremonies, stuttering a little. He was silvered and portly, down-to-earth, and he wore a beaded, bear-claw necklace. He read a simple poem by a cherished elder and then told it like it was:

"These five young men that we have here today . . . we're going to take this salmon down to the river and return it so that we may be able to enjoy this ceremony and the nourishment that it has brought to our people for, for, a lot of years.

"These young men have stepped up and volunteered to do this, and what is great about it, is that they're going to pass on to their . . . maybe one day their children will want to be a part of it. These young men are somebody, or some, that we can be proud of. To step up and do this. Younger people that, that . . . to see them and know what they are doing is a wonderful thing."

Rena jumped in, as a damselfly landed on her mottled hand and flickered away: "You young people—pardon me, Robert—listen to your elders, and you obey everything that your daddy teaches you. The tribal children, even the white ones . . . walk the straight and narrow, and when it comes your turn, and you're grown up, you can carry on, and your children, and your children."

Robert: "Before we do go down, there are some people who I would like for us to honor. Their names are in the program, so I'll just go ahead and read them. Let's keep them in our hearts and think of their families.

"Honoring friends in passing," said Robert.

Donald Allan, Jr.

Barbara Davis

Robert Davis

Delbert Rainville

Deagan Season

James Sturgeon

Thomas Sturgeon

Florence Watkins

Melissa Wheelock.

In the coming year, Rena Cox would be added to the list.

Three boys gripped the tray, and two followed, and they led us through the tents and trailers, a quiet procession across pine and fir needle with the hum of generators all around. At the road, they looked both ways and went across to the river: their eyes on the fish, so the tray wouldn't tip; and on the ground, so they wouldn't stumble. Down the trail they shuffled, past stands of blackberry and stinging nettle, to a little graveled beach where Robert would speak of their common journey and responsibilities. I had been asked not to follow, not to take pictures, but I watched from above as they stood, knee-deep.

Behind me, the procession coiled into a circle in a small grove on the upper bank. Everyone held hands as Jessica spoke: "Grandfather, we ask you to protect these members of the tribe. We ask that you give them guidance, to lead them along a good path, a straight path. We ask that you give them the wisdom to face the tough choices that they're going to have to make in their life. And we ask that you give them a caring heart so that they can listen to it and make the best choices, not only based on what is right in the world, but what is right in their souls." Then the women began to sing.

The Cow Creek Band had lost track of much of its heritage during its fragmented years, but now it had come back together to re-educate its youth. In addition to the powwow, the band holds an annual one-day Culture Camp for about fifty kids, during which a batch of salmon is cooked the authentic way: on cedar staves over flame. As Teri described to me, a more traditional salmon ritual is also observed at the camp with a small audience on hand: "Everybody comes up and they take a bite of the fish, and then they put a piece on a cedar bough for their family, for prosperity and prayers. Seven or eight young warriors—boys that we choose—they'll dive . . . it doesn't matter what time of year. Each takes a bough, and they dive down to the bottom of the river and give it back to the river." They place the salmon under stones.

But today the boys simply slid the metal tray into the river and the ragged skin was given over. They were braves now, their feet in a flow that could only be believed, not seen. From my vantage point, I could see the carcass release a cloud of mayonnaise, leaving a milky footprint on the waves. This was milt in its own right. I imagined bits of orange flesh scattering downstream among the cobble to waiting crawdads and rootlets, and perhaps the fry of wild salmon. Slowly the skin drifted. It hung on a ledge, unhurried, and then gathered steam, turning over like an old plastic bag toward the Pacific, toward the casino. The women finished chanting, and the boys climbed back up the stairs of the bank and were greeted by whoops and cries; and the salmon carcass flashed vaguely silver as it ghosted past two lovers sitting, hip to hip, on a mossy boulder above the South Umpqua.

When the boys returned to the campsite, each was presented with a long object bound loosely in blood-red cloth. Cautiously, around the same table where the salmon had just lain in state, they unwrapped the fabric to reveal eagle feathers—some golden, some bald. In this day and age, only tribal members and certain educators may legally own such a thing. With serious eyes, in the thick sage light, they held the quills' hollow stubs and ran their fingers down the long vanes, smoothing and reuniting the barbs as if to make each feather perfect for flight. I wondered if they were picturing the six-foot wingspans of these birds—those whiteheads—that, on some rivers, gather by the thousand to scavenge the salmon that give themselves up to their progeny, to eaglets and boys.

Later I asked one of the boys, Scott, age twelve, from the nearby town of Riddle, if the salmon ceremony was important to him.

"When they honored me with the eagle feather," he replied in a voice that approached silence.

Did he have somewhere in mind for it?

"In my dresser," he said.

"Seems like a safe place," I replied.

"I got'a go . . . ," he said.

I asked another of the new braves, Trevor, if he was going to enjoy the salmon dinner that was on its way that evening. His cousin, DJ, there by his side, took the words right out of his mouth: "He doesn't like it. He likes fish sticks."

Trevor nodded solemnly.

At last, the time grew near. The salmon had been lifted by human hands at least fourteen times: Once when they were sorted at the hatchery. Once after they were killed. Once when they were unloaded at the casino. Once in its kitchen. Once to hitch a ride to the powwow. Once to be mayo'd. Once foiled. Seven times over the pit, in the hands of Barry McKown. Now they would be lifted at least twice more. Once so that their flesh could be harvested, mounded for the buffet; and one last time, on the tines of a fork.

They had remained an extra hour on the grate and finally cooked, and now Barry and others carried the radiant packets to another table. A box of latex gloves awaited volunteers. This time, I wanted to lend a hand, to earn my keep for the weekend. Unwrapped from the aluminum and its own blue-gray skin, the flesh was at first too hot to touch and shrunk the plastic around our sweating fingers. But we managed to loosen the meat, with the help of spatulas, all of us reaching onto the table. Hands working over these lemon-adorned bodies, beautifully destroyed, their bones minted at sea. "Those aren't bones," said Jessica. "Those are Indian toothpicks." We plied and piled those pastel chevrons, mortared with ocean fat, onto silver trays to serve to the tribe at large. The sweet, clean-smelling steam rose visibly in the warm air.

For six months, following a strong, or perhaps weak, moment just after New Year's on a subway platform in New York City, I'd been an honest vegetarian. But as I picked over the soft fish, my fingers lifted an orphaned piece to my mouth. First one stray flake. A minute later, a second. Then the floodgates opened, and it was all I could do to keep my lips off the sticky gloves. Even in death, these salmon were the antithesis of dry, and tasting them, I felt, like everyone else present, that here was our own flesh come back to us, with a hint of mayo. Those boys may have stood more firmly in a spiritual flow—in the runoff of these mountains—but I felt something like a current then, as dinner was announced over the PA and people queued up in a long line with their eager stomachs, their aluminum camp ware, and their ancestors on the tips of their tongues, if not everywhere overhead.

Discovering Anna

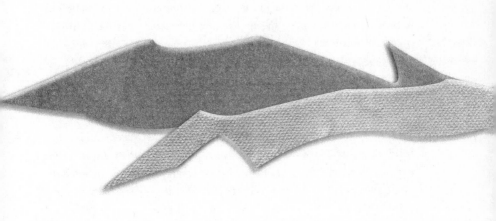

As a child, I set out in search of hummingbirds. Probably this wasn't ordinary for a boy, and I was fortunate, indeed, to have come into a large and varied country south of San Francisco, a dry sea of chaparral up against—and sometimes over—the deer fence, a landscape with plenty of perches to map and explore: yellow sticky monkey flower, poison oak, coyote brush, ceanothus, and the miscellaneous exotics of the garden.

⌒⌄⌒

Anna's hummingbird was the species. *Calypte anna*, an abundant resident of the Pacific Slope. Even in winter, they're here, outside the rain-slithered window, hovering in the green, shifting from branch to branch to probe for insects, pillaging spiders and their stuck prey with hardly a quiver. A hardy bird. All but a few North American hummers migrate, and come spring, the orangish Allen's would also arrive suddenly from Mexico to spar for territory. But he's smaller, less frequent, and, for now, another story.

Who is Anna? She was the duchess of Rivoli, Anna Masséna. Her husband, François Victor Masséna, the duke, was an amateur ornithologist with a vast collection of exquisite bird skins that eventually included the "type specimen" of his wife's namesake. One imagines her as striking: light on her feet, a fine dancer; draped in stones that caught and refracted the candlelight of nineteenth-century France; a touch spoiled, certainly. She became the official mistress of the household to Eugénie, the wife of Napoleon III and last empress of France. Earlier, in 1828, Audubon visited Anna and observed that she was "a beautiful young woman, not more than twenty, extremely graceful and polite."

Apparently, the duchess was admired also by René-Primevère Lesson, a surgeon and naturalist, surely related vocations. It was he who named the species. In 1822, he left France to serve on a four-year trip around the world, during which he saw and described many of South America's most brilliant, pip-squeak birds. Rounding Tierra del Fuego, *La Coquille* (an apt ship name, *The Shell*) went as far north as Peru and then cut across the Pacific to Tahiti. Lesson gathered specimens of all kinds during his circumnavigation and brought them home to study, label, and slip away in drawers. For years, he labored to prepare the zoological chapters of the expedition's official record, and afterward he produced the world's first monograph on hummers: three volumes of luminous, hand-colored plates. It was in preparation for this work that he chanced upon an unrecognized skin in Duke Masséna's collection.

~~~

Hummingbirds, you should know, are found only in the New World. There are more than three hundred species, but only fourteen commonly breed in North America. Fittingly, Christopher Columbus was the first to write of them, in his diary: "Little birds . . . so different from ours it is a marvel." Not long after, Pope Leo X was presented with a preserved skin that is thought to have arrived inside a chest of curios and treasures, a gift from the king of Portugal in 1514. The bird's chin may well have been as ruby as the robes of Leo's cardinals. Europeans were captivated. They thought it half insect. *Oiseau-mouche,* the French said, "fly-bird."

From the age of four or five, I kept little cardboard jewelry boxes in a spare bureau in my room. Each full of findings: sand dollars, oak galls, feathers, owl pellets jutting with rodent bones. A cabinet of curiosities, its drawers squeaking with the weight of geodes and fossils. If you have a sharp eye, these enthusiasms start to build upon themselves, or maybe it's the other way around. Soon others begin to notice as well. For Christmases: a rock tumbler, a seashell book, a chemistry kit (with beak-like forceps and pipettes), a microscope, binoculars, and many other useful tools I can no longer recall. Also for Christmas: more discarded gift boxes, each ready to be neatly packed and fitted into the display.

Calypte. It comes from a Greek root that means "to cover or conceal," and a male Anna's hummingbird does peer out from beneath a hood, a veil of iridescent red. All hummers glow with refractive color. Their most lustrous feathers don't hold colorful pigments, only black melanin. Instead, a number of wavelengths reflect—rebound—from various depths in the feather's crystalline nanostructure so that, when the angle is just so, their crests and troughs align, synch up, "constructively interfere." These parallel strands of light are the intensification you see. Grind up this bird's iridescent plumage and just a small, ashen pile of dust will remain. When the angle of reflection is wrong, his crown looks entirely black; but if he turns and stares straight at you, then *flash*—like a red sky glancing off a sea. He can raise or lower his feather tracts, adjusting and directing this aggressive hue based on his mood. What is he hiding under there? His crown patch blends into his scaled gorget, which looks like chain mail guarding his voice.

In memory, I'm standing on our lawn with a view across the valley to a crest called Skyline, where the Pacific fog would pour over the redwoods many evenings and waver like a white tide. From the grass, in the late-afternoon sun, I'd watch the excursions of the male Anna's, especially his courtship dive. Only the males perform this elaborate dance, the most extraordinary of North American hummingbird displays: He rises slowly, elegantly, into the air, pausing to warble before he's lost to the viewer more than one hundred feet overhead. Too high to see, a speck in the platinum sky. Then he plummets—or rather, powers down at fifty-five wingbeats per second—only to brake sharply in front of a perched female and sound a piercing note: a sharp *pik* made not with his voice, as once thought, but with his two outermost tail feathers. They cut the air like a bullroarer. Quickly, he circles back, rises again. How many times have I watched him perform this "J-shaped dive," as it's called, this loop-the-loop before an inconspicuous female, "the object of the display" down below in our Australian bottlebrush? Hundreds. Thousands, in my mind's eye.

But what you really must know about Anna's, about the male specifically, is that he's the only North American hummingbird that truly sings. The males of other species make sharp, aggressive *chip* notes full of desire, and those of the other *Calypte* species, Costa's, do let forth a simple ascending-descending "song." But just Anna's have a bona fide tune, something to almost whistle along with. It's a squeaky warble, rodent-like. But I find it adorable. Even today, while walking a city street, I will hear his raspy singing, perhaps from a tree growing in a planter outside of Safeway. Any young sapling off the sidewalk might hold one belting at its tip amid the waves of traffic noise. Sometimes I'll stop midstride, point to the air, and say to a friend, "There's an Anna's." Wait a few seconds, listen. "There." I seem attuned to high frequencies, like a dog. Once you zero in on a sound, you're not likely to forget it. The key is learning that other language naturally, when you're young and receptive. I've heard it takes a teenager an average of seven times to commit something to memory. For an adult, often more than twenty.

Several years ago, researchers from China ventured to California to investigate *Calypte anna*'s voice. They recorded forty-seven males in April and May at the Golden Gate Bridge, Golden Gate Park, Lake Merced, and Filoli Gardens, an old estate in the hills not far from where I grew up, a place my mother sometimes would visit for botanical watercolor classes (fine-tipped brushes, a few hairs sipping pigment). Each bird species' song has its own rhythm and syntax: In Anna's, the researchers—the listeners—found thirty-eight syllables in all, which build phrases like "bzz-bzz-bzz," "chur-ZWEE," and "dz! dz!" to name just a few. Each male knew an average of five syllables and shared some with his neighbors—the "tutors" he learned from—helping the birds to know and negotiate the ever-shifting boundaries of their territories, while shaping neighborhood dialects and the overall melody.

Of course, the genus *Calypte* also calls to mind Calypso, "she who conceals," the sea nymph who held Odysseus on the island of Ogygia for seven years. Shipwrecked and washed ashore, he didn't object to her company at first: They shared a bed. But after a while, Odysseus grew homesick and, wishing to leave, spent his days pacing the shore with tears in his eyes. Zeus sympathized with Odysseus's plight and dispatched Hermes, his messenger. When Hermes flew into Ogygia, he marveled at Calypso's garden: "Round her cave there was a thick wood of alder, poplar, and sweet smelling cypress trees, wherein all kinds of great birds had built their nests." But Calypso wasn't pleased with his tidings that she must let Odysseus go. "You gods," she cried out, "ought to be ashamed of yourselves. You are always jealous and hate seeing a goddess take a fancy to a mortal man, and live with him in open matrimony. . . . I got fond of him and cherished him, and had set my heart on making him immortal, so that he should never grow old all his days." But it was decreed. Her human must continue on.

Sixth grade brought new sophistication. My parents gave me a Nikon camera, a tool to record. Quickly I borrowed my mother's telephoto lens and stole into the brush of the backyard, into the manzanita with its small, white, bell-shaped flowers. Or I hunkered down below the prickly bottlebrush, with its profusion of crimson stamens—one of the hummingbirds' favorites. My arms would grow shaky as I tried to steady the heavy lens and remain alert. Sometimes I'd lose focus, let my eyes wander. But I was always listening: *bzzzzzzz*. Then I held my breath, trying to still my camera and that blur of wings. Glossy prints, color slides: At night, the projector poured light through life on the white wall of my room, filling it with red and green. *Click, click,* I shuffled through. Many out of focus, off-center, but how could even one be thrown away? They held information. The sequence was crucial. I filed them away in plastic sheaths, in binders and boxes, as if to seal them off from dust. Someday I'd study them more carefully.

Recently, high-tech cameras helped calculate the speed of a male Anna's in his J dive: fifty-eight miles per hour. Relatively speaking, that makes him the fastest animal in the world at 385 body lengths per second—almost twice as fast as a peregrine falcon in its free-fall stoop. When a male Anna's turns in front of his female counterpart perched below, he experiences ten times the pull of gravity, more force than fighter pilots experience in their jets (they travel a mere 150 body lengths per second). The Berkeley graduate student who took these measurements, Christopher Clark, also captured a composite of one male's dive out of the clouds: a long necklace of images, downstrokes and upstrokes that taper into a glide before the hummer flares its tail, braking rapidly. Calling forth. Clark journeyed to a nearby park, a retired dump—always a good place to bird—in order to perform his initial experiments on *C. anna*. He snipped the two outer tail feathers from a netted male, released it, and then watched as the bird dove: *whiff*. The silence astonished him. Later, he put tail feathers in a wind tunnel to further explore their "aeroelastic flutter," air trembling around those trailing vanes as if past the reed of a saxophone. He'd proven the source of the species' dive note. But in point of fact, it had already been ascertained in 1940, when another inquisitive soul mounted the outer tail feather of an Anna's on a thin strip of bamboo and, like a kid, whipped it (*pik*) through the air.

Photo by Christopher Clark

Slowly I discovered the males' routine singing perches. The highest lay beyond the lemon bushes, over the deer fence, and above a tangle of scrub. My father built us a tree house twenty feet beyond our latched gate, in an oak leaning precariously above a small, dusty canyon with a horse trail running through. Two parallel planks ramped up the trunk. From there, a few wooden boards nailed to the bark served as a ladder to a deck with railings. Above the ravine's steep slope, we rode currents of air. The canopy of oak leaves was our roof, broken with light, projecting green across the platform. In middle school, in pursuit of hummers, I would creep nervously out onto a twisting branch, hold tight with one hand, and with the other take photographs of a male Anna's, half in shadow, crooning at the edge of the tree. It was as if he were looking out for signs of land.

Myths of origin, flights of fancy: The town where I was raised is named for Don Gaspar de Portolá, a man born in Catalonia, a soldier for the Spanish army in Italy and Portugal before he was named governor of Las Californias from 1768 to 1770. Between those years, he led an overland party of sixty-three soldiers, missionaries, Native converts, and muleteers north from San Diego to scout for mission sites on the coast, and hopefully find the fabled port of Monte Rey. But they didn't quite recognize Monterey Bay, and after three and a half months, instead came to a perch on a coastal ridge where they saw a great swath of inland water. They called it Estero de San Francisco, thinking it an arm of the then Bahia de San Francisco (now Drakes Bay), so christened by another explorer in 1595. Though they didn't realize it at the time, in fact Portolá and his party were the first Europeans to glimpse what lies inside today's Golden Gate. It's funny, I could have sworn I was taught that Portolá first saw the bay from the crest of my town, but actually he summited the ridge about twenty miles farther north, as the hummer flies. This much, at least, I hope is true: Saint Francis of Assisi, the patron of my home port, once turned to his companions and said, "Wait for me here by the way, whilst I go and preach to my little sisters the birds."

In school, you are asked to relish facts, to pick apart passages, to hold them up to the light, arrange and cache them away. But they only live as you do. Not surprisingly, we often dove into California history, learning about the Franciscan missionaries, the gold rush, and the local Native Americans. The Bay Miwok called hummingbirds *kulúpi*, or "messenger." Their glittering feathers were woven into baskets and ceremonial headbands. Some tribes said—say—that it was Hummingbird who poked bright holes in the ceiling of night. The Ohlone, who also lived by the bay, tell of how Hummingbird's agility and cunning returned fire to the world: In the darkness, Eagle sent him on an epic mission to the underground Badger people. He was to reclaim flame for all the other animals. At his approach, the Badger people selfishly covered their glowing pit with a deer hide, but Hummingbird saw a slit of light where the arrowhead had originally passed. He poked his narrow beak through and clasped an ember, carrying the spoils away. But before he could tuck the coal under his armpit, his throat kindled and began to burn, long and slow, and even now in my backyard.

Europeans first thought the hummingbird a phoenix that could rise from the dead. The Spanish friar Bernardino de Sahagún, translating from the Aztec language in the sixteenth century, dubbed them *pájaros resucitados*—"revived birds." The origin of this myth is understandable: At night, or if the cold is severe, hummingbirds fall into a torpor, a temporary hibernation to save energy. The body temperature of an Anna's plunges from its normal 107 to as low as 48 degrees Fahrenheit, just enough for life. Then, two hours before dawn, the hummer begins to stir and vibrate its wing muscles, shivering to warm its blood for about twenty minutes before flight. Alexander Wilson was one of the first to note this trick in his 1831 *American Ornithology; or The Natural History of the Birds of the United States, Volume Two*. One cold day, he prodded a hummingbird in a shaded wire cage—not an Anna's, but a ruby-throated, the only hummer found in eastern North America. "No motion whatever of the lungs could be perceived, on the closest inspection," Wilson recalled, "though, at other times, this is remarkably observable; the eyes were shut; and, when touched by the finger, it gave no signs of life or motion." So Wilson carried the bird outside and set it in the sunlight, where it must have glowed even in its stillness. He continued to watch: "In a few seconds, respiration became very apparent; the bird breathed faster and faster, opened its eyes, and began to look about, with as much seeming vivacity as ever. After it had completely recovered, I restored it to liberty; and it flew off to the withered top of a pear tree."

Calypte. Before he left Ogygia, Odysseus confessed to Calypso that he thought she was gorgeous, more beautiful than his wife. Still, he wanted desperately to go home. She sent him sailing with bread, wine, and water on a raft he'd built from the island's largest trees. He navigated by the stars, those holes poked in the sky. It took Odysseus ten years, all told, to return home from Troy. Homer doesn't mention any children between him and the sea nymph, but other classical accounts imagine one or two. Now I find myself wondering: Did René-Primevère Lesson, upon discovering this bird new to science in the duke's collection, suddenly recall the story of the sea nymph? Did he name this creature for Anna Masséna in patronage, or with secret affection? Did he picture and long to see the bird floating, singing, above these green-brown hillsides of a land he would never visit?

On the fringe of Silicon Valley, in the late 1990s, we learned to make clunky websites, feeling like pioneers. Eighth grade. If my memory serves, each of us picked a different animal, and mine, of course, was Anna's.

We searched field guides, textbooks, and other soon-to-be-extinct genres for vitals, and then we bracketed this natural history between simple code. Several of my best snapshots I scanned and cropped with precision; my friends, working on behalf of cheetahs and blue whales, couldn't so easily include original art. And when I walked through the tinted-glass doors of the cool, cave-like computer lab into the warmth and glare of the school's courtyard, how satisfying to hear that familiar voice from the oaks or the wisteria trained on a trellis overhead. That website is lost now, ether. I'm not entirely sure that it ever went live.

A further education: At school, there was this girl, Moriah. Several years in a row, she won a blue ribbon at our science fair for *Anna's Choice I, II,* and *III.* Her motivating questions: Does Anna's hummingbird have a feeder-color preference? Do Anna's hummingbirds prefer feeders with perches? Does feeder exposure influence feeder choice by Anna's hummingbirds? Her explorations and answers didn't light my fire, but I admired and envied her immaculate poster board (fastidious, she was—or her parents) and her brilliant array of glass bottles hung upside down, each with sugar water. Anna's hummingbirds, not surprisingly, are highly territorial. I hear she's a geneticist now. It's a shame that I was too proud, or shy, to talk to her about our mutual fascination with a creature whose heart can beat over a thousand times per minute.

To know, to understand. Our desire is for more. New heights: They're always within reach. Stay, Odysseus. Several years ago, scientists anesthetized and performed minor surgery on a small flock—a hover, a glittering, a tune, a shimmer, a bouquet—of Anna's, all caught near Los Angeles. They inserted .08-millimeter silver wires into their breasts, into the pectoralis major, in vivo, and flew them in a controlled setting— inside a box—to discover, by way of electromagnetic waves relayed along the wires, how their muscles are selectively fired depending on the intensity of flight. The scientists dialed back the air density to make the birds increase their exertion and lengthen their strokes. They also put tiny harnesses around the birds' scintillating necks and attached them to weighted chains, to measure their ability to lift increasing loads. Cameras recorded it all. "These results suggest that hummingbirds recruit additional motor units (spatial recruitment) to regulate wing stroke amplitude but that temporal recruitment is also required to maintain maximum stroke amplitude at the highest wingbeat frequencies." I must confess I have only the foggiest notion of what this means; in essence, first more muscle fibers contract, and then they do so more quickly. But just imagine all those birds hovering, pulsing, at the end of their silver tethers.

Leaving a basketball game once, I spotted a male Anna's lying in the gutter among the curled oak leaves of winter. How old was I? It slips my mind. But from the rush of spectators heading toward their cars, I stepped off the curb and scavenged it with the pinch of my fingers. A little gummy mass, stuck with bits of sand, had spilled from its feathers and congealed: not an oxygen-rich red, but darkness, the way its hood and gorget look in life when the bird turns its head and the blaze disappears. I placed the bird in my palm and carried its weightless body home. It was the first time I'd held a hummingbird. On the desk in my room, I laid the specimen on a clean sheet of watercolor paper and bent my lamp low. With a black felt-tip pen, I ruled out several inches and took photographs of the bird beside the ticks of the line. I measured those wings, its compact emerald body, its slightly decurved bill: discovered and documented such fineness. Then I set it—him, because of the scarlet crown—on a windowsill outside the laundry room, in a lidless Tupperware so air would circulate (a hint of sulfur). A few weeks later, he was gone, as if he'd flown away. I was surprisingly hurt. Sick to my stomach, even. Around and around the driveway I wandered, looking, wondering if he might have blown again to some far corner, some island or pile of leaves.

Safe passage is not guaranteed. In 1670, the governor of Connecticut, John Winthrop, delivered an emblem of the Americas to the English naturalist Francis Willughby with a note: "I send you withal a little Box with a Curiosity in it which perhaps will be counted a trifle, yet 'tis rarely to be met with even here. It is the curiously contrived Nest of a Humming Bird, so called from the humming noise it maketh whilst it flies. 'Tis an exceeding little Bird, and only seen in summer, and mostly in Gardens, flying from flower to flower, sucking with its long Bill a sweet substance. . . . I never saw but one of these Nests before; and that was sent over formerly, with some other Rarities, but the Vessel miscarrying, you received them not."

All that time I spent watching Anna's in the backyard, I never found a nest. I knew *his* territorial perches, each and every twig, but I was never quite on *her* wavelength. In contrast to the male, she is quiet, gray and green, truly concealed except for a small, irregular iridescent spot on her throat, a discreet touch of flare as if a gift from him. She is very independent: Anna's hummingbirds don't pair. The male doesn't help rear. But there's this early note, suddenly, a rekindled memory: Six or seven years old, I'm at a park when, at my feet, I chance upon a half-dollar-size nest on the lawn. A thimble of down, woven with lichen scales and spider's silk—the prize of any collection. But it never reached the bureau; it must have foundered, slipped out of my hand somewhere between the grass and the car, and I'm remembering it now for the first time in a long while.

Then this fact, not at all strange, but wonderful: In the first half of the twentieth century, Anna's didn't range north of Southern California. In winter, they wandered into Arizona, but not much farther afield. Since then, however, their numbers have boomed, right alongside California's great water projects, which gave rise to orchards, to urban and suburban gardens with flowers when all else is quiescent. Eucalyptus also proliferated, which the birds love (rightly so, since the tree shares their name, *calypte*: Its tasseled flowers are well "concealed" by a hard cup). Sugary feeders grew in popularity as well. Thus Anna's irrupted elsewhere, tied to us. They've colonized the whole coast and are now across the border into British Columbia. Onward and upward, into their dive.

How often our strongest memories seem to take shape at a fence line, some edge: I am standing in the lemon bushes below the adobe retaining wall of our tiered vegetable garden. The lemons are soulful, aromatic, so close their waxy, puckered surfaces fill my peripheral vision. But I'm peering through the fence's wire windows into a wash of sinuous, drought-tolerant scrub taller than me. I'm birding, I imagine—looking out for California quail or thrashers, and Anna's. Suddenly one arrives from behind, startling me. So close, the camera useless. I hold my breath as if submerged, while the hummer dangles inches from my face. I imagine its black, wiry toes clasping the freckled bridge of my nose. It twists slightly, an ornament hanging, shifting as if to see its reflection in the glistening leaves. It hangs there. Then *whir*.

As it turns out, a male Anna's dives headlong toward the sun. They have evolved to do this, we think, so that their vermilion reflects exactly into the eyes of the beloved or the intruder. The biologist who first wrote of this azimuthal tendency carried a stuffed specimen mounted on a wire into the Berkeley Hills and held it up, like a lightning rod, for the living. I imagine him crouching as a hummer bears down. "In this circumstance," wrote William J. Hamilton, "the orientation of the dive was easily determined. . . . The effect is one of a tiny ember, suddenly descending upon the observer, growing in brilliance and dimension as it approaches, to burst with a pop as it passes over." They are such jealous birds, extremely competitive. When I was a boy, three or four Anna's at a time would dart overhead, chasing each other, rattling their high-pitched calls like cans trailing from a marriage car, like sirens. They seemed to call to me as they defined and furiously defended their territories in a yard I would eventually learn wasn't really mine. Then, exhausted, that hover or shimmer of birds would fall away to separate twigs, each to sing. The Spanish, as you know, gave up California. The tree house oak fell down. Our actual house was sold.

What's odd about a hummingbird is that, even as it lingers, you antici-pate its departure. Sometimes this distracts you from the present. My hometown is this way, now. Small, green, zipping through. Iridescent, from certain angles. I still visit. There are still photos, boxed away, of a shadowy figure framed among the foliage. But it's unlikely I'll live there again, where the dust and amber light are so entwined as the sun lifts from the oaks and, across the valley, withdraws into the redwood crown of the Santa Cruz Mountains. Such is the J dive of discovery: Again and again (and again), there is also loss. But more is found.

Gone Rogue, or Suck It Up

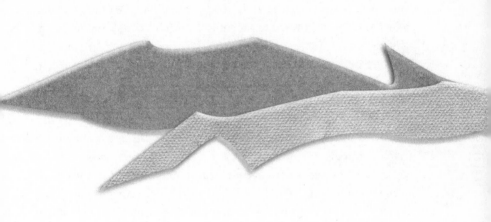

On a cloudy Sunday in July, traveling through southern Oregon with no firm destination in mind, I peeled off I-5 into the small town of Gold Hill, whose streets declare its history by way of businesses like The Miner's Roost (the local watering hole) and Nugget Auto Parts. I was hoping for a glimpse of the town's latest boom, but was unsure of what I would find, or if anyone would talk to me. Swing a left on Upper River

Road, and you trail the rough-hewn Rogue River through a neighborhood of unpresuming ranch houses until the pavement gives up, turns
to dirt, and skirts buffy Bureau of Land Management hills studded with
oak. There are thirty-seven miles of free mining access along the Rogue,
and this stretch is apparently far from panned out: About forty suction dredges were moored along the willowy, rocky banks or anchored
midstream.

Most were idle. In suction dredging, a diver wields a hose underwater to siphon up the riverbed and its potential pay dirt, but the day
was cold, intermittently drizzly, and most of the miners—dredgers, I
should say—were at home, or in their comfy RVs, rather than in the
49-degree water. But I encountered a few. First, Dave, a silver-haired
man in dripping red hibiscus board shorts and neoprene booties. He'd
just dragged his six-foot dredge off the river and, with the aid of a local
friend (whose name I didn't catch), was corralling its tentacular parts
into his truck bed, cursing and groaning, and clanging; the thing looked
like a hybrid of a go-kart and a central vacuum. He lived in Newport,
a town on the coast, and had to drive the four hours home to return to
his day job on Monday.

"You writing a book?" Dave asked me, after a minute, as he shoved
his gear one last time and slammed the tailgate. "Cause you're sure
asking a lot of questions." He'd only just peeled off his wetsuit, and
I suppose it wasn't the best time to nervously ask about dredging, or
whether he was getting into any gold. Probably he just wanted an Irish
coffee.

"Not yet," I said.

"Well, do you want to know what I call my mining business?"

I nodded.

"Mining my own business."

John, a guy from Portland, was friendlier and voluble, more forth-
coming. Sort of. He was mining "somewhere on Earth" "about fifty
minutes away," and he looked flat-exhausted, his eyes slightly blood-
shot, maybe because he'd spent the previous afternoon belaying his
dredge ("a giant underwater hookah," he said) down a remote cliff
to his private claim. That's how mining rights work on most Oregon
rivers; the open access on the Rogue is rare. John had blown the day

off to recover and, already, scout fresh stretches. I ran into him along a rippling bend with a view of Lower Table Rock: one of two sheer volcanic mesas that rise like curtains above the agricultural Rogue Valley. "Is it worth it!" he called out, optimistically, to another miner who had surfaced midriver to rest on a boulder like a mink, a small universal dive flag—red with a white diagonal stripe—waving over his dredge. "Sorry, I can't hear you," the miner shouted. Fifty-fifty that was true.

To and from Gold Hill, you drive along a deep, unhurried stretch of river lined with black oaks, their lobed leaves as large as hands, their limbs hung with lengths of Spanish moss that sway in the breeze like the scraggly beards of miners past. Lots of dredges here, tied across the way, opposite the dusty public road—the more difficult to steal. When I pulled over to stand waterside and gaze at the Rogue's laconic gloss, I heard a rustling from the bank's willow and grew tense. John emerged. "Oh," I said, "it's only you." We stared at an enviable "party barge," as he called it: an extra-large, stand-on-top dredge that, as it happened, four men worked together, ferrying across each morning in an aluminum canoe. Rain began to etch circles on the river's dark vitrine. "It looks calm," John said, before returning to somewhere on Earth. "But it beats the shit out of you."

Shortly after, down a rutted blackberry- and poison oak–infested spur that traced the Rogue, I stumbled upon a turnout with a white pickup backed toward the river. A man in his sixties peered around the cab, short but broad-chested, in sunglasses and a ball cap, his T-shirt as gray as his hair. Taking me in, Ray apparently decided I wasn't much trouble; the day before, he later told me, another miner's truck had been broken into—thus, Ray now had a machete handy. "I'll wave this around and yell, 'Come on!'" Ray mused. "They'll think I'm crazy"—true—"and won't mess with me." He and his thirty-nine-year-old son, Jason, had flown to Medford from North Carolina to join a friend and fellow prospector, Bob, for a few weeks submerged. Unfortunately Ray had been sidelined on the bank for sudden health reasons, which is probably why he entertained my questions: He was bored. Each time Ray spoke, the silver caps of his lower molars winked.

Soon Jason and Bob came wading in, nearly hypothermic, carefully floating the contents of their sluice box in a plastic tub down the placid side channel that led to the narrow beach and pickup. It was time to pan the results of their first, short dredging test at this locale: Ray's job. In his yellow-and-black dry suit, Jason reminded me of a NASCAR driver (the hall of fame is in his hometown, he noted). Stocky and strong, with a russet moustache and Carolina drawl, he and his older brother had recently inherited Ray's construction firm, Southern Pools, which also builds waterslides and tennis courts. No wonder the family dredged: They often worked underwater, scrutinizing walls for cracks and leaks. Bob, on the other hand, was a retired dentist from Bend, several hours away in Oregon's eastern high desert. I had to stifle a quip about an "extractive" personality. With a soft, giddy laugh, and a patient way of explanation particular to the best of doctors, he wore a blue three-piece wetsuit, dubiously patched at the knees after all the time he'd spent kneeling in rivers.

Bob seemed skeptical of me; as he wrestled his neoprene and toweled off with genuine *brrr*s, I could tell he was sizing me up out of the corner of his eye. Here was a tall, strange "writer" who'd emerged, without warning, from the woods. But Bob warmed up, literally. The sun finally began to cast off the woolly marine layer overhead as Ray got down to business. He sifted the gravel from the dredge's sluice into a green plastic pan, filled it with water from the Rogue, and began to "agitate," first swirling and then rocking gently to suspend its sediments. The heavy gold, if there was any, would quickly wriggle to the bottom, to the pan's circular crease.

With each motion, Ray let a bit more sediment wash off the pan's edge, in tiny sips, until only black sand was left. Finally, he spread this heavy, ferrous content thin across the top of the tilted dish, illuminating "the color" underneath: an arching constellation of gold flakes and dust, and a few modest "pickers"—pieces large enough to pick up with your fingernails. By now, the goose pimples on Bob's biceps had vanished; sunlight was flowing generously. It was an eighth of an ounce, roughly two hundred dollars' worth, a promising outcome for a half-hour's dive. "So you want to see some mining, huh," Bob said, shaking my hand, and his head, as they drove off for Medford. "Okay, see you tomorrow." I ended up staying four days.

~~~

Here's what sucks: A lawn mower–sized engine, which produces an equally brain-rattling sound, sits on pontoons and pumps river water through a tapering tube named for Giovanni Venturi, an eighteenth-century Italian physicist, which creates a powerful jet. Right below the dredge, the venturi is joined to the diver's hose (tough corrugated plastic, about fifty feet long), so that this rapid stream enters and converges with the motionless river water already inside this would-be vacuum. Because this incoming flow is so speedy, by the laws of physics it has a lower pressure: Voilà, water is drawn up the diver's hose to fill this relative void, transforming its whole ophidian length into a vacuum strong enough to suck up the riverbed—and anything else that fits. If a diver's hand strays near the nozzle, it's pulled right in. Luckily this is more startling than dangerous. This is the Bernoulli principle at work, the same that dictates that air moving slightly faster over the top of a curved wing will generate lift.

On the pontoons above, the siphoned slurry comes to light and rushes over a reclined sluice box, cascading out its rear in a continuous blink of cobblestone, gravel, and silt. Tried and true technology—the forty-niners used them—a sluice is simply a trough laddered with rills and layered, now, with modern collection surfaces (green felt carpet, shaggy blue "miner's moss"), which create miniature eddies that cause the heaviest material to fall out of suspension as it flows by. Bob's engine was 6.5 horsepower; it burnt a gallon of gas every six hours; brand new, such a rig costs about five thousand dollars—or about four ounces of gold.

"What's that?" I asked, of a sunken metal cage with a thirty-pound rock lodged inside. I was standing knee-deep in the Rogue in the green fishing waders I keep handy. Jason was wearing earplugs to dampen the motor's noise, but apparently he could hear me.

"That's our anchor," said Jason. "It's also the size nugget we want."

The guys had caught wind of a formidable lump found, not long ago, at the foot of the three-foot-tall crude concrete diversion dam that we hurdled coming to and from the pickup. Reputedly, a savvy prospector had spotted this nugget while floating on his stomach and peering into the froth at the dam's base, below the smooth spillover. "A miner's tale," said Jason: possibly true, probably exaggerated. But I was already itching to borrow a mask and go snorkeling.

"Most of the big stuff's gone," Bob told me, noting that successive gold rushes are the story of evolving technologies that make sifting out ever-smaller particles, from more-difficult-to-reach places, increasingly economical. "Occasionally someone will luck out, but it's like winning the lottery. This fine stuff was inconsequential to those in the past, or they didn't have the techniques. A hundred and fifty years ago, there were nuggets just lying here. Those miners would laugh at us. They just threw this kind of material away. They wanted large, gnarly pieces, and they found them—but they still had to work hard." These days, suction dredgers go so far as to send their seemingly barren, panned-out black sand to online companies, which process it for microscopic gold and send back a check.

To begin dredging, you have to crack into the river bottom with a pry bar, excavating a chink in the "hard-pack" of its floor, an unwitting fortification. The thing to remember about gold is that it's *six times* heavier than the average river material (silt, gravel, cobble), making it fairly easy to locate—almost always, it's wormed its way to bedrock, as far down as possible—but arduous to access. During major floods, streambeds are broken apart, swept up, held aloft in a muddy turmoil. As the flood wanes, first gold succumbs to gravity and drops out; then other stones, and finally the lighter sediments, which, under the current's pressure, fill the nooks and crannies to form an extremely compact riverbed: hard-pack. Much of geology, in this fashion, is an incomprehensibly vast game of *Tetris* that is both sluggish, on the order of vanishing mountains, and torrential. The pan in Ray's hands, in fact, is a microcosmic version, a controlled flood: Lighter sediments are suspended; ponderous gold sinks straight to the bottom. Thus a suction dredger has to dive not only through water, but also through the riverbed to reach the impenetrable stone where gold waits. All this must go. It's bedrock or bust.

Supplied oxygen through an air compressor, hose, and (as in scuba) a mouthpiece regulator, Bob took the day's first subaqueous shift, wavering like a blue shadow in the ceaseless Rogue as Jason and I stood by the floating dredge, ten feet away. Underwater, the diver sweeps his mammoth hose across the vertical wall of the "hole" he's made in the riverbed, methodically slurping up the conglomerate of the hard-pack, enlarging the pit. While one hand manipulates the nozzle, the other clears rocks that might jam the hose, much like a point guard uses his free arm to protect his dribble. To help lighten the drag of the hose in the current, its midsection is tied to a rock or log upstream. Whenever possible, the diver overturns big stones, sometimes with that pry bar, because beneath you tend to find pay dirt.

"Bob's definitely moving a rock!" Jason once yelled in my direction over the motor's roar. "See how much more he's breathing!" Big bubbles rose like jellyfish to the surface and revolved aimlessly, lazily, toward the Pacific before they released the former contents of Bob's heaving lungs. His pickup had a winch for moving large boulders, but there was no need here. These stones were reasonable. Elsewhere they can be the size of a pickup. Down below, you also "pop the cracks" in the bedrock with a chisel, breaking up the stubborn aggregate of gravel wedged in these natural rills, where gold hides. Another time I watched as Jason battled one of these stiff sunken seams. Only the tip of his crowbar stirred the surface, in violent jerks. It was as if he were trying to plant a strange flag, or poke a hole in the Rogue and drain us all away.

The diver depends on the vigilance of his above-water partner, "the tender," who carries a metal pole. The tender is like a shepherd with his crook, who looks on wisely while the sheepdog, underwater, does the real work. But as Bob explained, if you somehow get pinned underwater (by the rock you're undermining), and you don't have someone above to rescue you or call for help, your only hope is that the gas feeding your air compressor runs out soon, sparing you the torture of having to wait hours to drown. The tender's main job, otherwise, is to make sure the hose doesn't clog, which it tends to do right at the venturi's attachment. When the outflow sputters, the tender becomes a plumber and plunges with his rod. Ram, ram, ram. Stones rattle out.

This is the story, in fragments, of what's known as Oregon. All sorts of hues and forms: Ochre red. Serpentine green. Once, a stone with white quartz ridges, making it look like a mammoth's tooth. Caddis fly larvae in their tiny bead-like tunnel-homes, built of dark sparkling gravel, in which the bugs metamorphose before they float to the surface and fly. Behind the dredge, the rocks collect in humps that, in a shallow river like the Rogue, over time thankfully provide the tender (and his interviewer) a perch out of the cold water. Periodically Jason and Bob swept these piles flat with their gloved hands, both to clean up and make room for more tailings. "Back home, we get good money for this kind of landscaping rock," said Jason. "But it's everywhere out here." A geologist could really wile away, or even catalog, these hours. I just marveled at the colors.

In 1851, two mule packers readying camp about fifteen miles south of Gold Hill led their animals to drink from a clear, nose-tingling stream. Looking past those tired hooves, the men glimpsed "color" in the water's gravel, that fateful harbinger of riches or ruination. This was five miles west of Medford before Medford was a twinkle in the eye, on a tributary of Jackson Creek, which drains to the Rogue. Miners soon welled north from California, many of them Oregonian settlers who, only three years earlier, had dropped their plows in the Willamette Valley and forded the Rogue when cries of "Eureka!" were heard from the Sierra Nevada foothills. Now, quickly, a Table Rock City was nailed together. It was shortly renamed Jacksonville, in honor of its gold-bearing creek, and became the seat of a new Jackson County. It was the largest town north of San Francisco.

Gold Hill, meanwhile, is named for the illustrious pocket that was turned out here above the Rogue in 1860, a year after Oregon joined the Union. One of the two richest lodes in state history, this white quartz vein is said to have been twenty-two feet long, ten feet deep, less than a yard wide, and so intricately laced with the precious element that much of it couldn't be broken up with a sledgehammer, because gold is so malleable. Another miner's tale, but something close to the truth: Seven hundred thousand dollars of gold was reportedly extracted—at $20.67 an ounce. That's forty million dollars, at today's prices. The partners of the Gold Hill mine felt so magnanimous as to present a specimen from their fabulous vein to the Washington Monument, then under construction. A piece of the Rogue hills remains buried in that marble obelisk, a symbol of Oregon's arrival, worth, and inclusion in the nation.

This first boom busted by the early 1860s, but another would arrive before the turn of the century in the form of hydraulic mining, wherein teams of men, some of them Chinese, hosed entire hillsides into flumes using "dictators" or "giants," as their cannon-sized nozzles were dubbed. Those alchemized the Rogue, so to speak, rendering it pure brown, choking downstream wetlands with silt and dramatically reshaping the landscape. But on the whole, Oregon's gold production was modest aside other western booms. Those golden days served mainly to jump-start more vital, lasting business.

But history tends to bubble to the surface. Directly across the Rogue from Bob, Ray, and Jason's operation was the Gold Nugget Wayside, a pull-off and picnic ground on a road that runs toward Crater Lake. Beneath twisting, tawny, smooth-trunked madrones, an interpretive sign endeavors to explain "The Lure of Gold." Naturally, along this bank another small dredge was tied, hidden among the verdant aquatic grasses, with a tiny Jolly Roger raised above it like a flag over a miniature golf hole. Its owners were fair-weather dredgers for sure, appearing only on warm afternoons, when there was sunshine aplenty to rejuvenate the skin, and soul. They were either locals, or they weren't having much luck. "You can always tell when a dredger is getting a little bit of gold," Bob said, "because he works a lot longer and harder."

Our nearest neighbors—James and Henry from Chico, California— were anchored behind a boulder one hundred yards upstream. James was a rather sizable fellow with a walrus mustache. Like most fluvial miners, he was a seasonal laborer: During the winter, he delivered fertilizer in tanker trucks to Central Valley rice growers, and during the summer, he dredged. In his neoprene hood and sleeveless wetsuit—sleeveless!—he looked like a mallet-wielding superhero. Or a headsman. His machine was a rumbling two-engine beast that put Bob's to shame: not quite a "party barge," but aspiring. To meet Oregon's regulations, he had added an attachment to his nozzle reducing its diameter from six to four inches. But who knows what remained attached underwater.

I saw this duo at work just once, my last day on the river. As Big James readied to dive in behind his boulder, he contorted his elephantine hose over his right shoulder like a lumberjack hauling a log. Man, did that thing suck. It absolutely mowed. Henry played the role of hopeless sidekick. No good at diving, he tended the dredge in a death metal T-shirt and a faded-rose The Ohio State University cap, from which his long silver-and-black ponytail flowed. After a few hours, they took a long break to sun in lounge chairs, savor potato chips, and drink Shasta soda, while James's 150-pound wolf-husky mix sat calmly at their sandaled feet with gelid eyes. Said James, "We're getting into it a little bit."

Our other neighbors, Pete, a tall muscular cop with a strong, stubbled jaw, and Matt, a thin, live-wire carpenter, were from Wisconsin. Their accents proved it. They were still learning the mining business, but had pushed ambitiously into the river's alacritous middle, hoping to be duly rewarded. Sounded, however, as if they had just been thrashing in sand. By their own estimation, their three-week excursion had been a bust; now they worried about what they would tell their wives after the long drive home. But each morning, Matt dutifully waded in behind the diversion dam to their spot with his wetsuit peeled to his waist, a steaming coffee in his hand, a cigarette in his lips, and his empty neoprene sleeves trailing reluctantly in the still water. It was Matt's truck that had been broken into, so he'd propped up a sign, scrawled on cardboard, on his dashboard: *I've purchased a Game Tracker camera, so if you're reading this, I already have your picture.*

Dredging is exhausting work; you have to fight the current, the hose held in its sway, and those tumbling stones. But it was the chill that was driving these guys from the Rogue. Flowing water relentlessly sloughs heat from the body. Sinewy Matt, for one, was having real trouble staying down for long. And after a two-hour session, Bob would stagger forth, his face off-white, puckered, and creased through his hood's oval window. He'd doff his weight belt onto tailings, those worn geologic bones—*splash*. "I worked around those two rocks," he reported to Jason after one typical effort, his teeth chattering. "But there are three or four more I left for you. There's good pack underneath. My goal was to stay in two hours and move those rocks—which I did."

Then Jason would sink into the Rogue, where, in his NASCAR colors, he looked like an enormous drowned yellow jacket. Increasing amounts of duct tape began to appear on this "dry" suit, which, fortunately or unfortunately, he had borrowed from his brother. By design it was tight around the neck and wrists to prevent seeping water. But real tight, a size too small. Those cuffs resembled rubber gaskets, and he kept tugging at his collar like it was a tough day at the office, which happens to be what he and his father liked to call the river ("No one's telling you when to arrive," Ray told me, "or when to quit"). "Wow," Bob once said when Jason surfaced. "You look purple." Jason could only nod; language was still thawing in his throat. Having barely warmed up himself, Bob then donned his weights once more, spit into his mask and sloshed it clean to prevent condensation, and holding the regulator, said, "Put me in, Coach. I'm ready."

Southern Oregon was unsettlingly overcast and cool. At least for July, when normally the Rogue Valley is sere and baking. "It's not supposed to be like this," Bob grumbled. "In California, it gets to be 110 degrees in the canyons. The sun pours straight down and bounces off the walls, but underwater, it's just perfect. You mine with no top on then—only a mask."

When Bob first learned of dredging, he traveled to the remote town of Happy Camp, just south of the border in California, and took classes offered by a mining club known as the New 49ers. The original fortyniners had named Happy Camp during its heyday, for obvious reasons; it sits on the Klamath River, Sasquatch territory, a famed and tumultuous gold stream that plummets through northwest California. Bob was immediately smitten with the activity. "I'm pretty kinetic," he said. "I like to work hard, use my body. Dredging sounded like it would do that, and it does. But when you're down there, it's quiet. For me, it's a meditative experience. If it wasn't so cold, I could stay down pretty much all day. And at the end of the day, you might have some gold."

Apart from the noise, suction dredging does have much of the spirit-lifting appeal of other outdoor recreation. Mid-Rogue, the view was of timbered hills and volcanic bluffs, the mist curling off the water each morn, the river gliding over the retired diversion dam behind us. As I loafed beside the rig, I glimpsed all sorts of creatures: With backswept wings, an osprey crashed into the river just in front of us and stole a trout. Red-breasted mergansers whistled upstream in a blur, like arrows shot from a bow. Blue and orange rafts drifted past, and their paddlers studied us as if we were the wildlife (*What the hell is that machine?*). When I queried Bob as to his most memorable dredging moment, he told me about mining the Salmon River in California one August afternoon. Exhausted and alone, he'd surfaced from hours of suction to find thousands of dragonflies swarming overhead. Swooping in pursuit of some insect. Diving toward the river, almost touching it. "I hadn't looked up in three or four days," Bob recalled. He lay on his back on the bank in the hot evening and, as if still at the bottom of a pool, watched them flicker and click across the hazy blue.

Bob first met Ray and Jason on the Salmon, a tributary of the Klamath, when they bought neighboring claims in 2005. Ray and Jason bought three, actually, and all told have invested about one hundred fifty thousand dollars in this enterprise. You're right: That's a lot of gold dust. But time is ostensibly on their side. When they began mining twenty years ago, gold was worth less than three hundred dollars an ounce, yet on my first day loitering in the Rogue, it climbed past sixteen hundred dollars, for a time. Theirs is not only a hobby, but a long-term investment that will pass from father to son. A hundred ounces, or so, would pay off their speculation. Once, on the Klamath River, Ray and Jason, and a few other friends, whisked up seven ounces in two weeks.

Unfortunately the guys bought into the Salmon at precisely the wrong moment, at least in the short term. A year afterward, a local Native American tribe, the Karuk, along with several prominent environmental groups, brought suit against the California Department of Fish and Wildlife, claiming that suction dredging was hard on rivers and fish, and that the environmental impact review was insufficient. The historic territory of the Karuk, "The Upriver People," is the Klamath drainage, and their modern headquarters is Happy Camp. They caught the ear of Sacramento and, in 2009, Governor Schwarzenegger suspended all suction dredging until a new review could be undertaken.

"This does nothing to an ecosystem," Bob argued. "Now, in the old days, when they raped and pillaged, and killed the Indians, there were real problems." Indeed. Nothing does nothing to an ecosystem (let alone a culture), but I understood Bob's frustration and at times imagined the dredging I saw as a weirdly localized storm that swept up riverbed and laid most of it right back down. In a six-hour workday, the average dredger sucks up two to three cubic meters of riverbed, or about twenty to thirty wheelbarrow loads. On the upper end, that means ninety miners/divers might collectively plow up an underwater football field, end zones included, in a couple months' time, which by rule is the length of the dredging season in Oregon.

The largest concern—the rallying cry for opponents—is the well-being of wild steelhead and salmon, which nest in riverbeds and are especially vulnerable while spawning. On the whole their populations are terribly reduced, less than 10 percent of what they once were. Having to contend with dredges could tip some exhausted salmon over the edge, energy-wise. And there are other complications: A female salmon spends days crafting and curating an artful nest in river gravel with her tail, in which she deposits her life's work, a kind of translucent, oily gold. Possibly she might select dredge tailings for her spawning bed (though she is very discerning), but this gravel is mobile, a booby trap that would destroy her roe. Sediment plumes from dredges might also fill the porous interstices of salmon nests, suffocating or starving eggs.

In its new review, however, California Fish and Wildlife concluded that suction dredging's environmental hazards are "less than significant" if precautions are taken. The cavities that dredges scour in the middle, or "thalweg," of a river are filled by normal winter floods, while marginal piles and potholes are likely to vanish after several seasons. If dredging is prohibited during times of salmon spawning, incubation, and early emergence—as it already is in Oregon and California—these complications are probably avoidable.

But when I stumbled upon Ray, Jason, and Bob, the moratorium was ongoing, much to their irritation, because the state wasn't sure it could afford to enforce regulations. Thus history had repeated itself: Once more, California miners were trickling into southern Oregon, this time driven not by a boom, but a ban. Our hero/headsman Big James, for another, owned claims on the granite-strewn Yuba River in the Sierra— more river, he said, than a team of twenty could work in a lifetime. Yet here he was in Gold Hill, outcast with his gorgeous husky and death-metal Henry.

Here's a confession: I myself have a history of mining on the Rogue. Several years ago, I was fortunate to spend six months living within the eighty-four-mile "Wild and Scenic" stretch of the Rogue Canyon, where the river is deeper, more brooding; the boulders a slick ebony, and the size of ten-passenger vans. This is to the west of Gold Hill, ocean-bound. My solar-powered cabin sat on a five-acre meadow that was a steep, fifteen-minute walk from the river, and two hours from a grocery store via bumpy, winding BLM roads. No other lights in the canyon. Just Jupiter. Below the porch stood a few apples trees, a sagging barn, and a garden with an electric barbwire fence to slow the bears.

Along this part of the Rogue, you can find rusty twelve-inch-diameter piping riveted together long ago. From mossy, maple-umbrellaed creeks, it stretches diagonally across the hillsides. In the late 1890s, mule trains packed it in so that teams of miners could wash out and sift through whole banks with their "dictators," with stream-fed hydraulic blasting. Now, inside one length of pipe, I hid a camp chair for my evening reading at a local cove. There were battles in the canyon during the Rogue Indian Wars of 1855–1856, instigated, not surprisingly, by the influx of miners who displaced and massacred the Takelma, "Those Along the River." Lesser outrages also occurred: The original homesteader on my meadow, Dutch Henry, is said to have killed his mining partner (watch out, Big James). Two of them, actually, on separate occasions. Along this wild section of the Rogue, you still can find remnants of claims, cabins, and cable used to winch gigantic boulders, as well as the rare musket ball.

In Grants Pass for groceries one day, I bought a plastic pan for a few dollars at the Armadillo Mining Shop, a place of regional renown where you can buy bumper stickers that read "Earth First! We'll Mine Other Planets Later . . ." and any other mining paraphernalia, including suction dredges. Back at the homestead, I then borrowed a plastic colander for a sieve and a screwdriver for a pick. Both of which I subsequently wore out and had to replace. If you're only panning, the best strategy is to "snipe the cracks," which is also basically what Bob and Jason were doing underwater with their pry bar: On bankside stone, look for cracks perpendicular to the stream's flow. A river is the archetypal sluice box, after all, and during floods these cracks act as natural rills. Water eddies in these crevices, drops its gold. Scrape them clean and sift. Swirl your pan carefully. After more hours than I'd like to admit, I had gleaned a tantalizing pinch of dust and a few sizable flakes. The largest I named Africa, for its shape.

When I hiked out from the homestead in December, fifteen miles east along the Rogue, the vial that held my gold collection shattered in my backpack. I might have burnt it to recover the dust, like dredgers do the felt carpet and "miner's moss" from their sluice boxes at the end of each season; but I'm afraid my backpack was worth far more. So I shook out the big, outer pocket into a nonstick frying pan and swirled away the sand once again. Africa, and all the other micro-continents, were still there, beckoning.

I've always been somewhat bemused by the fact that this element, this shininess, was the standard to which our financial systems, and so much of history, were once pegged. What could be more arbitrary or frivolous? It's a pliant metal, that's all; it would make for a particularly soft hammer. Allegedly, all the gold "recovered" to date in the world would cover only a football field four feet deep, which is astounding. But on the other hand, why isn't such scarcity a knock against the stuff? Yet I must admit that I am who I am because of gold, not least because I am a Northern Californian. My fourth-grade class, like many others, field-tripped to the Sierra foothills, to "Gold Country," where not far from Sutter Mill we panned our first glinting flakes from a long wooden trough that was definitely stocked, like a man-made pond is with fish. This was my heritage, I understood. The Niners were my football team.

So when, as a twenty-four-year-old, I caught my first wild flash, borne by the Rogue, it was about time. And the appeal of gold, I see now—or I would speculate—is above all illumination. It afforded us light long before we named the oil we indiscriminately burn "black gold," or dammed rivers like the magnificent Rogue for electricity. Pressed into leaf, it is relief from shadow, reflecting the day or a candle around corners into dark, interior spaces. To an extent, our attraction is simply biological. The eye gathers light and won't be denied.

In elemental terms, that's what Ray, Jason, and Bob also pursued: In the semitranslucence of water, something ignites the retina. "If you ever stick that nozzle on bedrock and see gold, you're the first person to ever see it," Ray told me, with a hush in his voice. These guys weren't in it for the money, not really. "I don't know any miners that are making a good living," said Bob, though, it's true, they probably wouldn't tell you if they were. Chasing light was the goal.

For darkness is a cold prospect. Along the Rogue in Gold Hill, I slept in my Jeep at night, shoveling my camping gear to one side so that it formed a precarious wall on the verge of collapse, like the hard-pack Bob and Jason siphoned away underwater. I'd have slept in the open air, but rumors of marauders crept into my head. Miner's tales, probably. But I'd also heard that it was illegal to camp by the river, which I wholly believed since no one seemed to try. Nowhere else was free and convenient, though, and it was an easy commute to my temporary "office." So I compromised, keeping a tidy camp in my car; imagining that I might have to make a sharp excuse, if not a getaway, from the end of this muddy access road, hemmed in by trees and brush, and beside railroad tracks that, after midnight, returned me suddenly to consciousness with a flood of sound.

One night, as I was eating pasta and boiled squash from a pot, the beam of a sheriff's spotlight swept through the spindly madrones of the Gold Nugget Wayside just across the river. My nerves tingled; I put out my headlamp, feeling illicit. But I was thankful for that searchlight as well, because I couldn't say who else kept to these woods. Tweakers and survivalists, marijuana growers and desperate writers. They might imagine something like gold was hidden in my glove compartment. Briefly I felt the attending shadow that, ironically, most prospectors have known. I locked myself in at night. I located my pitiful Swiss Army knife. And come morning, I boiled my coffee and looked forward to mining, wondering if those flakes Bob, Jason, and Ray intercepted were from the same mother lode as those I'd gathered a few years earlier, sixty miles downstream.

There are degrees of hard-pack. The hardest is so dense, so compact, it requires a "blaster" to loosen up the riverbed—a mini "dictator," in essence, that jets water like a dentist's spritz, except it will break your skin. Occasionally gold will lie atop so rigid a layer, because it acts like a cobblestone street. But on the Rogue, the miners were demolishing "semi-hard-pack," which the hose easily devours. Good thing. In suction dredging, how much gold you recover is directly tied to how much riverbed material, or "overburden," you have to tunnel through to arrive at bedrock. The deeper the overburden, the more burdened the miner, but we were standing on just two or three feet. "You can't get much better than this," said Ray. "Well, you could get better—you could find the damn vein."

But much of what the guys were recovering was "flood gold," which is like the static that might distract a listener from the real signal. For here's another truth: Gold is every goddamn place in the Rogue Valley. Erosion broke it apart and carried it downhill, and incredible floods flushed these particles swiftly downriver, en masse, spreading traces clear across the flood plain over millennia. Over eons. "Your valley used to be your mountains," Ray explained, pointing to the top of the ridge, "and your mountains used to be your valleys." Gold was even wedged in the random boulder marooned by the left rear wheel of Bob's pickup, which all week Ray vigilantly guarded. One afternoon, just for kicks, he kept busy by scraping one of the boulder's grooves clean. He panned out several flecks of gold. "What I really need for sniping the cracks is a dental tool," said Ray. "Bob's got plenty of those, but not here."

Nothing illustrated the inversion Ray described better than the Rogue Valley's iconic Table Rocks. We couldn't quite see these raw volcanic buttes from the dredge, but they were nearby, towering like monuments around the bend. Ten million years ago, the whole valley had been a sandstone plain, way above our heads. Then lava covered it all a hundred feet deep, in the process blocking and filling a prehistoric river—some ancestral Rogue—and sending its water skyward as steam. Gradually, other generations of rivers washed this volcanic layer and the softer sandstone below it to the ocean (creating the next sedimentary plain, offshore and now ready for uplift). In the Rogue Valley, only a few of the deeper, more durable meanders of that fossilized river were spared: the dark horseshoe formations rising eight hundred feet above us; the Table Rocks.

So it goes with gold: It flows downhill, with mountains. Rain, snow, ice, wind, and streams are the original "dictators." The richest prospecting stories, not all of them apocryphal, are of cowboys tripping over outcrops of gold in plain sight, which by legend is how the Gold Hill pocket was discovered. In theory, you could locate such a lode by painstakingly sampling hillsides for loose gold and, ever so gradually, triangulating—following the fan of erosion to its concentrated source. Barring that, you have to recover gold that has entered a waterway. Dredgers and all other placer miners rise each morning in search of those lucky crevices and boulders where dreams settle and disappear.

Idling in my waders, I realized fishermen and miners have much in common. Where fish lie to save energy, flakes are likely to rest, too, say in an eddy behind a boulder (Big James knew just where to throw in his hose). You also learn to "read" the river for possible deposits: A miner becomes the mind of gold. But unlike fish, gold will forsake deep, quiet water for the shortest course to the sea, depositing, for example, in the shallows of a river bar, on the inside of a bend. It has momentum. "Like things go in the same direction," Bob explained. "If you find lead, sinkers and nails, hubcaps, that's a good sign." Deposits of sand, like the Wisconsinites were battling? A red flag. Lighter material isn't apt to follow the same line as gold (which is also why the lighter stuff flows out of the sluice). The ideal for a suction dredger is to discover an accessible "pay streak"—the path gold has traveled and settled—and follow it into the sunset.

You know the river's finally giving up its gold when the tail water of the sluice begins to churn a light, warm brown. This tint represents the finest of silts, a thin layer pancaked between bedrock and the rest of the riverbed. This is the burial ground for valuable metal. On the Rogue, this clayey stream came in pulses, like a heavy exhalation, as Bob or Jason cleared the gray "overburden" to suck up this final, soft connective tissue. To my eye, this plume of ancient particulate—a fragile interstitial realm subjected to light again, at long last—dissipated about thirty feet downstream. Jason also described a rare orange mud, found beneath certain and unknowable rocks, that he's learned almost always harbors gold. Whenever he spies it, he gently sets the nozzle beside the patch and tickles it like a chin to see "the color" revealed as the sediments are whisked up the hose.

As I lingered in the Rogue, the water's chill gradually seeped through my waders, and my long underwear, and I found myself basking in the warm, mildly intoxicating exhaust of the dredge. Yet there comes a moment—thigh-deep, having borrowed a mask so that you can plant your (now-tingling) face in a rushing river to study the blue neoprene humanoid slurping up the very wet earth upon which you stand—when you realize it's time to suck it up yourself and take the polar plunge.

Rogue Aquatics, a dive shop, sits beside an open field with a *Hay for Sale* sign on Crater Lake Highway, just north of sprawling Medford. They rent only seven-millimeter wetsuits, about the width of a word like "frigid." Such insulation makes sense, given that the Rogue drains off the snowy shield of Mount Mazama—the stratovolcano that blew its top seven and a half thousand years ago to create Crater Lake—and into Lost Creek Lake, where it flows from the lightless bottom of the reservoir's dam to recommence the 215-mile journey to Gold Beach, past the homestead where I lived. But the mere act of wriggling into one of these wetsuits—past two bulbous ankles, over leg hair—boils the blood. From the rack, I then picked out a hood with a flamboyant orange, red, and yellow racing stripe. A pay streak.

"Just be careful you don't rip the knees to shreds," said Bob, the next day, "or you'll have bought that suit." His own were epoxy-patched to a ghoulish extent.

While Jason took his turn as waterdog, Bob offered up more sound advice: "Don't worry about messing up—we've already messed up everything you possibly could." "Sometimes I mow down the wall of hard-pack with two hands" (he made a motion, here, like a gangster brandishing a machine gun). "You want to hug the bottom, so you don't get sucked away." "Tuck the air hose into your weight belt so the regulator doesn't pull out of your mouth." "I pay close attention to my body, and I try to stop when I start making bad decisions." "Don't look up, or the current will blow you out of the hole." "If a rock gets jammed in the nozzle, you'll just have to bang the shit out of it, to get it loose." Over the last several days, I'd watched Bob dislodge several vicious blockages from the midsection of the dredge's suction hose; each time I had imagined a wrestling match, to the death, with an albino anaconda.

When Jason emerged looking purple as usual, Bob helped me strap on a forty-five-pound weight belt and eight pounds of ankle weight, which counter the current and the neoprene's buoyancy. I cleared the regulator—*puff, puff*. Then, I porpoised. The water percolated through my tight wetsuit surprisingly slowly. But instantly, it was clear that this was the closest to being a river—to bedrock, as some like to say—as I had ever come, and probably ever would. As my adrenaline coursed, I looked out at a drowned field of stone. You might not know you were in a moving fluid, except for the undulating patchwork sky, and the bits of sand and wood that whirl past. And the unrelenting force.

The drone of the motor was almost completely snuffed out; mainly I heard the *shush* of the water, the clicking and clacking of stones, near and far. Of mountains peregrinating. Swiftly I crawled into Jason and Bob's working "hole" and tried to catch my bearings. Looking to my side, I studied two small spotted fish, salmon fry perhaps, finning in place as if in an aquarium. For a moment I tried to emulate them, to lie still in my hold, to embody their contours. Miners often say that fish come right up to their armpits and eat the ambient bits of life they dislodge, the algae and larvae. Their kingdom was peaceable. My charge was to dismantle this refreshing, pacific view and send it up the hose, which hummed subtly electric.

As soon as I tried to start mining my own business, however, it was a different story. Picture a long, lean fellow using the fingertips of his left hand to cling to a horn of blue-green bedrock, as if it to the saddle of a bronco, while straining to drag a heavy corrugated hose (a lasso?) forward with his right. Quickly my view was clarified: A river of this nature couldn't care less for a human being; it measures one's strength and, unfailingly, finds it pathetic. Staying productive *and* in place was nearly impossible. So was seeing through the fog that consumed my mask, the rivulets that ran like snakes down the inside of its glass, and the silt I stirred up as I toppled the neat cobblestone wall of overburden the guys had entrusted me with. And when Big James revved up his beast again one hundred yards upstream, I was swamped by his plume of particulate. Bob's form of "meditation" seemed a pipe dream then. More than gold, I sucked compressed air.

But I did experience several minutes, over the course of about forty-five, when I was suspended, like a proper aquanaut—like gold during a flood—in that place that Bob, Jason, and Ray loved. The learning curve is steep, but suction-dredge mining is a sport of strength, grace, and nerve, as well as destruction. In fact, to picture a body, then, might be to miss the point. One retreats toward the embryonic. Descends. The practice begins to soothe. You slip into a "time warp," as Bob claims. As if it were true: Time is like a river. When I finally emerged, Bob summed up this phenomenon about perfectly: "You came up and said, 'Five more minutes,' and twenty minutes later, we ran out of gas."

As the air became thinner, I felt an alarming tug on my mouthpiece: the anaconda! No, it was just my tender, Jason, saving me. I stood up, wobbled to the shallows, and unclipped the weight belt—*splash*—thankful to have survived the Rogue. Regaining my equilibrium, I returned to the dredge to eyeball my catch. Flipping over the rubber flap that streamlines the hose's outpouring over the sluice, I stared down at the rills. Among the black sand in the grooves, there lay at least one conspicuous flake I'd unwittingly sucked forth. Plain and glorious, a speck. It seemed to wink at me, to become my mind: Ah, Nick, you can do better. Go ahead, retrieve that red gas can. Hell, why not just buy your own dredge? I'll help you pay off the gear in a few weeks, or days.

A Guide to Coyote Management

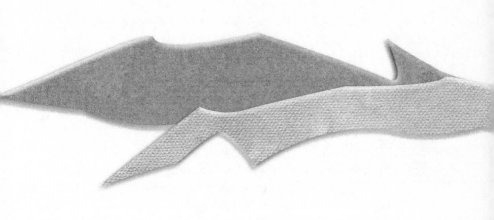

Coyote can be detrimental to any number of natural resources, including livestock, watermelons, pets, and the economy. He is known to tiptoe about places he shouldn't, like airport runways and Walmart parking lots.

Occasionally Coyote takes larger prey, small ungulates such as fawns, lambs, calves, and foals. The concern of this document, however, is primarily with domesticates; Bambi—another of the First People—is on his own.

Let's keep in mind that Coyote warrants management in part because he feeds on calves by eating into the anus or enteric region. The coprophagic son of a bitch absolutely loves it. He can't wait to do it again. "Up yours!" says Coyote—his mantra.

If you find a dead lamb, calf, or foal and suspect Coyote, first examine the neck and throat for subcutaneous hemorrhaging. Typically, bites to a dead animal do not cause hemorrhaging, although this diagnostic is unreliable if the carcass is old or widely scattered.

Among animal tracks, Coyote's are smaller than wolf, smaller than large dog, larger than fox, smaller than yours, perhaps. His footprint tends to be more ovular and compact than dog or human; his step is light and regular, and always just ahead or just behind. Quiet, he is near.

By law you are allowed to kill Coyote year-round, if you have a hunting license. But as a gentle reminder, night-shooting Coyote with a spotlight is illegal in most states. Wait for a full moon, when he'll come creeping along like the milkman, drunk on cheap beer, pissing morning glory, looking to sleep with your daughter and your dog.

Before we go any further, remember: The focus of managing Coyote should be damage prevention and control. Termination of Coyote and his legacy is not the goal. *Coyote was here!*

To start, a good fence goes a long way against Coyote. Until he decides to go around it. Watch him tightrope the barbwire along the highway just for show. He keeps a stepladder in his back pocket, a shovel up his coat, and the sun on his raggedy shoulders. He squats on top of fence posts, marking his miles.

His digging may be discouraged with a length of barbwire along the ground. Climbing may be deterred with an electric overhang. With enough barb and current, anything may be deterred, maybe even Coyote. He will be kept busy scavenging the souls of other animals, such as the migrating antelope strung up across the range.

During a one-year study involving one hundred Kansas sheep farmers, seventy-nine sheep were taken by Coyote while in their corrals. He laughed all the way to the bank and thought about number eighty. Why'd he stop? Coyote despises round numbers. He hunts them in his sleep.

Yet only four of those kills occurred in lighted pens. Circling or blinking lights further increase the chances of frightening Coyote away. Alternately, use blue or red lights, because Coyote seems *less* afraid of those particular tints. Take aim as he steps into the color and begins to dance with his shadow, whispering to himself. Stay steady. Look through the sights to his stare.

Here's an idea: Keep the radio playing all night. Coyote can't *stand* talk radio, AM especially.

But beware, he digs most music. He keeps a half-torn, life-sized poster of Lil Wayne on the wall of his den. Hip-hop one day, he can be pretty darn country the next. And rock-and-roll? Of course: Coyote's always ready to kick up some dust, to howl at some moon.

Park your pickup near the corral. Park it in a new place each sundown. Coyote will wonder: What is up with that restless Chevy? If that doesn't do the trick, then spend a night in the cab. What could be better than blowing Coyote away from a blind with headlights? What could be more comfortable?

Careful, though—fall asleep, and you might wake up to Coyote's bare ass spread wide across your dusty windshield, giving birth to the bobblehead on your dashboard.

〜〜

Two words: propane exploders. But make sure to turn off these noise-makers at sunrise. If Coyote is killing your sheep during broad daylight, turn to page 102.

In twenty-four Coyote-depredation complaints recorded during a two-year study in North Dakota, propane exploders were recognized as most useful in reducing Coyote's antics.

That is, until Coyote was simply "removed." Much more effective for a while.

But when he returned, Coyote lifted one leg and urinated exactly where he left off, in the thistle at the side of the road. His piss sprang into the air and took shape, becoming the first goldfinch. Perhaps this is why goldfinches have always flown a bit wobbly, dipping up and down like telephone wires.

Electric guards are a more expensive, even more effective option. They strobe brightly and blare horrible noises. Place your EGs high up on posts or trees to increase the range of their effectiveness and to prevent your irritable livestock from destroying them.

Unfortunately no external chemical repellent is known to dissuade Coyote from killing a sheep. None is repugnant enough. Coyote, after all, is made of scraps of squirrel fur and glued together with piñon sap. He lost his first self, skin and all, gambling at a truck stop. It's safe to say he's made his peace with foul smells.

If an effective repellent were discovered, surely the U.S. Environmental Protection Agency would never approve it. Hell, because of the EPA, a number of useful toxicants are no longer listed here. Blame Coyote. It was Coyote who began the environmental movement. He planted the first magnolia on the original Earth Day. He has sat for centuries, waiting for it to bloom.

～〜

During a controlled study, Coyote showed some aversion to high-frequency sounds broadcasted within one foot (thirty centimeters) of his ear.

"No shit," said Coyote, when later asked about the experience. He declined further comment. These words have often been misunderstood.

Try lacing a dead sheep with vomit-inducing salt. The technical term for this time-tested technique is "aversive conditioning." Colloquially, it's "gross." Coyote will turn mangy tail, to be sure, and trot to the edge of the field, faced squinched tight, tongue dangling. "Fuck you!" he'll yell out, and go in search of water.

Guard dogs can be effective against Coyote, depending on the terrain and experience of the dog. To raise a guard dog, select a pup from a good breed. Separate the young dog from its siblings after eight weeks and place it with sheep in a pen. Be sure escape is impossible. Let this socialization period last another eight weeks. Check the pup daily, but don't pet it. The dog's primary bond should be to the sheep. But first, before any of this, check to see that the sheep are not actually Coyote, wearing masks.

You should know, however, that guard dogs have been known to threaten children and cyclists. Consider whether you want to encourage such activity. In general, it's best to follow the ~~golden~~ rule. *What would Coyote do?*

Donkeys, also known as burros, are gradually gaining in popularity as sheep-protectors. Eventually, they may replace guard dogs entirely. A jackass's response to Coyote includes braying, exposed teeth, and a loping attack. They wholeheartedly loathe Coyote, though they are generally friendly to people. It may be because Coyote sneaks up on them through tall grass and rides them bareback.

Fact or fiction: More than one-fifth of Texan sheep and goat farmers rely on a jackass to safeguard their livelihood.[1]

Whatever. Llamas are the wave of the future. Someday they will replace donkeys as the best guard animal, because llamas befriend sheep within hours. Not surprisingly, 80 percent of ranchers who use llamas to guard their sheep are either "very satisfied" or "satisfied"—and that's the truth.

They're satisfied—are you? *Damn right—every night, for hours, if you know what I mean* . . .

No? Well, then try running your sheep and cattle together. Studies have examined the effectiveness of mixed sheep-cattle herds, and results show that Coyote kills fewer sheep. Strangely, no one knows why. Who *can* know why? Why is Coyote Coyote? *Coyote?*

The *o*'s in Coyote are for "ostrich." Let's face it: Coyote's just plain suspicious of novel, flightless stimuli. He buries his head in the sand, like the rest of us.

M-16? How about M-44. This spring-loaded booby trap shoots sodium cyanide into Coyote's open mouth when he clamps down on a baited capsule. Death occurs within seconds—dead serious. Unfortunately the effectiveness of the M-44 is hindered somewhat by EPA regulation in the interest of human and environmental safety. Additionally, it may kill your dogs.

Introducing the 1080! The 1080 Livestock Protection Collar selectively kills Coyote. Each twenty-dollar LPC holds three hundred milligrams of Compound 1080 solution. When Coyote bites your livestock's jugular—ha!—he punctures the collar and swallows a lethal amount of toxicant. No, Coyote—fuck *you*!

~⌒~

Even better, 1080 is a slow-acting toxin. Death is prolonged. Coyote will cry. Coyote will laugh. He will watch the vultures circle to his eyes. At the end, Coyote will like the way the flies dance on his skin.

Trapping? Some people succeed, though it's a lot of work. Hope is the thought of trapping Coyote.

A short list of items needed to trap Coyote:

1. A plastic bucket to carry items 2 through 10.
2. A No. 3 or No. 4 trap.
3. One seventeen- to twenty-three-inch stake for securing the trap.
4. A straight-claw hammer to carve a hole in the ground and drive the stake.
5. Leather gloves. Lord knows this is dirty work.
6. A burlap bag to kneel on for comfort. Keeps jeans clean, too.
7. Plastic sandwich bags to overlay on the earth, preventing dirt from getting under the pan of the trap.
8. A screen sifter for sprinkling dirt over the trap.
9. A rib bone—and not anything else—for leveling off the trap once set.
10. A jug of Coyote's urine to attract Coyote.

If you have allotted four hours to setting traps, devote three to looking for Coyote's signs, such as scat and tracks. Then, beat Coyote at his own game by using tricks to pique his intrigue. Place a long feather near the trap, for instance, and tickle his fancy. Or bury a ticking clock. Coyote will come around when it's time.

Don't leave scattered gum wrappers and cigarette butts. That's littering. Coyote knows it and knows better. He refuses to clean up after you.

~⌒~

Do place traps near carcasses or parts of animals. Leftover sheep heads are choice. Sheep heads really bring Coyote in. He's got a closetful at home.

Check the traps every twenty-four hours. No, check that. Check them once a week and save yourself some time. Let the Old Man suffer, if he's there. Better, anyway, to spend that time making sure that your livestock is not actually Coyote.

Unless, of course, you really want to shoot Coyote in the head. Unless, of course, you really want to hear Coyote sing.

The only Coyote fumigant currently registered with the EPA is carbon monoxide. Cartridges may be purchased to toss down Coyote's burrow. Quite possibly, it's the best way to have a "little chat" with Coyote and his family. This strategy is called "denning."

In classic denning, a hunter stealthily advances downwind of Coyote's home carrying a rifle or a repeating shotgun with heavy shot. He brings a dog to distract Coyote. He makes a call that sounds like the death squeal of Coyote's children. Coyote emerges and chases his tail to within short range of the unseen hunter.

That's when you pull the trigger. Pull it twice. Shoot the shit out of Coyote. Make a machine-gun sound through your teeth as you do.

Should he escape, drive stakes into the earth two inches apart at the den mouth and trap his pups. If he returns, shoot him, and then destroy his young. If Coyote does not return soon, destroy the pups anyway. Predation will often cease when the young are lost.

Where aerial shooting is legal and the den is in open terrain, wait until Coyote's little ones venture outside to frolic and doze in the sun for the first time, then decimate Coyote and his progeny all at once, like a hail-storm from an empty sky. Think "video game."

Denning is cost-effective. Bullets are cheap. Coyote will sell them to you in bulk. I mean come on, now. Don't be a sucker: Can't you see it was Coyote who invented the gun?

---

1   Answer: *Coyote wrote the question.*

The Garden of Earthly Delights

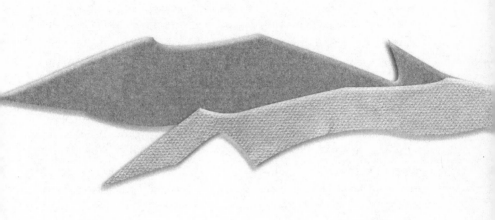

I had not expected to see all this mutilation. It would seem something of a tradition. Along this trail, the slender and old madrones, each and every one, are carved with the whims of passersby, like the arborglyphs of lonely Basque shepherds on aspen around the West. But do you know the madrone? It is the most human of trees. It has soft, smooth skin and often bends like a dancer twisting his or her myriad, dryadic arms. It exfoliates as it grows, shedding translucent cinnamon curls.

Bursting at its seams. This tree, with the milky under-color of the rind of a honeydew melon; which flares from nude to satin orange to fillet red; which, when mature, sometimes deigns to grow a scaly bark, rough and gray. The quintessence of umbilical, the mother tree: madrone.

Like revelers at a tavern table, we carve into this body, peanut shells underfoot. We have nothing, here, if not time and keys. Walking this trail to the top of Lower Table Rock near Medford, Oregon, you climb through black oak and glossy manzanita (some little cousin, by language, family, and texture) and then the madrones take hold in the nutrient-poor soil, where they thrive and wait for fire. That's where I begin to slow, noticing these inscriptions. Studying this proliferation of incisions. They build in number until you can't ignore them. Is this simple graffiti or collective art? A memorial or a gallery of horrors?

As a kid in California, I was taught to call these "refrigerator trees." Put your hand on its smooth surface, docents and teachers said. Press your cheek to it. Wrap yourself around it and feel the chill of sap close beneath the skin. As if magnetized, we are attracted. On this trail, we leave on them missives and sketches, the equivalent of (the desire for) family photos and shopping lists. Some trees are cut so profusely they are unreadable, sorely disfigured. Others only lightly marked. With smiley faces, penises, and other likeable vulgarities. With indiscriminant scratches, the passing glance of a fingernail.

But most of all with names and, especially, initials. We remind these trees and ourselves of our persistence. *SETH* scrawled as if with claws. *Inez. Emily. Noah. MICAH. MJ, KLB. IN* (or *HZ*, depending on how you read it). Pick any two letters. There is a multiplication of equations: *S + J, KD + MN. J + A 4 EVER. A + C = ♥. John + Chris. Shaila y Martin 2012* ➤ . . . unknown. Some of them so fresh, so viscous green, they might have been excavated this afternoon.

In a certain light, this place is violent (and how the light does shift as the clouds pass in a high wind, spotlights playing through the trees). There is, here, the pseudo-masochistic attempt to define a skin. Don't pretend you don't see it, this body. These trees are nothing if not figurative. They have accidental pimples and impromptu teats, swellings and cavities where the trees' flesh has died back or grown over broken limbs. And I don't doubt that some of these carvers imagined the skin of a madrone was someone else's. Or their own. We play at vivisection. Pretend surgeon. We are the tattoo or tortured artists. This walk is a reminder that stories (you plus me) are often scouring, the erasure of something. What is an essay, a book, but an incision into a tree?

But most carve not because the tree stands for the body—not consciously, I believe—but because it is softer than rock. These madrones present themselves, a supple medium to bind our love in its blindness. In theirs. There is such ultimate sweetness in such severe writing. This trail is a lovers' arbor, a linear bower with a long memory of holding hands. After all, the primary symbols here are plusses and hearts (♥), one kept safe in the bubble of the other. And maybe it should come as no surprise that before the heart symbol—that dimpled inversion of a teardrop—came to mean "love" in the thirteenth century, the shape already existed on heraldry as a representation of foliage. Of water lily and ivy, and in nearby forests, the sorrel that lays at the feet of giants.

There are, as well, the stars and crosses of sanctioned faith; but the difference between a plus sign and a cross, I see now, is a mere and tenuous extension. *Jesus Team A* is also carved here and there, and is everywhere implied, I imagine, for those who carry its letter in their hearts (faded scarlet, on a madrone). And nearby, the wavering circle-A of Anarchy. And as I near the summit of the trail, another svelte bole reads, *Dios te quiero mucho*, in a vertical cascade. But who is this *you*: God, or some other affection?

All these symbols, these letters, are a kind of arrow pointing to the self as well as to the top of Lower Table Rock, where you can stand on the edge of basalt cliffs (the remains of an ancient volcanic plain) and look out at the fertile Rogue Valley (a gouge in time). Where we will survey the S curves of the river and the pear orchards, their white spoiling blossoms, and see Medford in the distance, and I-5 cutting through (its traveling cars like the ants trailing up the trees). Mount McLoughlin is a snowy stratovolcano on the horizon. The red-faced vultures soar along the cliffs, below us, swerving hard in the warm updrafts that blow across our cheeks.

The madrone, I should say, was given its name by a certain Father Crespi on the first Spanish expedition into Alta California, the Portolá expedition, not far from where I grew up beside San Francisco Bay. He didn't care for its Native name (they had come to evangelize); and he didn't name it the refrigerator tree. Instead, this tree, which from Baja to British Columbia grows along the coast where it isn't too wet, made him remember the *madroño* of his homeland: the strawberry tree, with fruits that do resemble *fresas*. It is another in the *Arbutus* genus, a close relative of our madroño. And "The Strawberry Tree," you might be interested to hear, was also the original name for Hieronymus Bosch's famous triptych, the altarpiece now in the Prado and known as *The Garden of Earthly Delights*. In the early sixteenth century, paintings weren't titled; but in the catalog of the Court of Spain, this one from the Netherlands later became known as *La Pintura del Madroño*.

The left panel of Bosch's wild masterpiece is the unblemished paradise of Adam and Eve; the right depicts a wondrous but woeful damnation in an underworld of fire and demons. The largest, center panel overflows with a strange fantasy of nudes and fruits, either a picture of sin before the flood or, perhaps, if we read more generously, of paradise realized. No one really knows; we interpret according to our tastes. Pale, attenuated bodies lean against and pick from the strawberry trees; they hold and wear what look like cherries but which, to my mind, could just as easily be the edible berries of our madrone: blood-red and a favorite of birds (mostly tasteless to us). Bosch's people cavort and contort with each other and animals in a landscape of excess that, if you study their small faces, isn't necessarily the same as bliss. Nor is it meant to be.

Here I stand, alive, in the garden *del Madroño*. There are nudes all around, twisting. There is love, and there are the knives that lacerate it. That prove it. Off the trail, in a nexus of trunks, I even find one on the ground: a burnished, winking serration with a black plastic handle (the madrone's leaves also lanceolate and sometimes serrated). The knife is dropped or hidden, as if paramours were caught in the act and fled, leaving this evidence. Wanting to be found. As if they plan to return and continue their surreptitious, bawdy art. To cut their hearts out all over again. Or is it left here intentionally so that others, so that I, will take it up and add to the writing? I think of the third panel of Bosch's garden, a netherworld where knives loom, splitting a pair of gigantic ears and piercing hands and stomachs. Pinning us like moths. This realm is hinged to all the others.

Soon I begin to doubt whether particular windows into the gray heartwood are old letters or natural scars. Soon the innate patterns of bark, all checkers and curls, begin to pulse and blend with alphabet. I think a tree says *fear*, when it may say *pearl*. I think a heart holds *Dad*, and am disappointed when it is only *D+D*. Even in the moment of reading, on these trees is everywhere the reminder of growth and change. It teaches who would carve. All these letters will be distorted, subsumed, by new skin. Even the deepest shapes, the largest hearts, slowly infold. Most of these equations are quite literally left unfinished. Gradually the living phloem moves forward, like a lava flow always on the verge of cooling.

The biggest trees hold the longest memory, but it is the younger madrones that are ripest for paring, with their soft, herbal skin. Those near the trail's few benches (also carved) are especially vulnerable, most popular, and I wander through these groves, a voyeur with his instruments, his camera and his notebook. *Red- Neck*, reads one tree, and the words are so apt, so freighted, they rise (as they do over my head) to utter significance. Stacked one atop another, they are; the hyphen a copyeditor's afterthought. These words are a put-down and a coming-together, a declaration of identity. But I think also of all the necking that has gone on in places like this, from here to *4 ever*.

Down the trail comes a pair. She is, of course, a redhead, her shoulder-length hair windswept like the meadow (its ephemeral pools) atop Lower Table Rock; her eyebrows are pierced, a deflated backpack on her shoulders. He is wearing black-and-white camo shorts that hang below his knees, tall white socks pulled over his angular calves. His black T-shirt reads, *Fried Chicken and Gasoline*, and I don't quite know its degree of irony (how to read it). Down the trail, they flow, holding hands, a jaunt in their step and with the relaxed, faint smiles of electric companionship. Of a fulfilling date. On this unexpectedly sunny afternoon in late March, his exposed and chiseled triceps have burned rosy. Their necks are the pink of their affection. A hermit thrush in the understory sings with its ruddy tail.

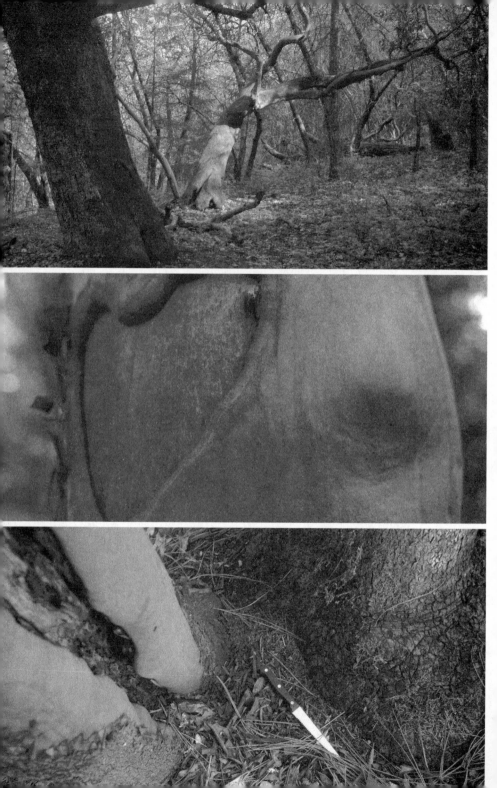

Photos by the author

The Carcass Toss

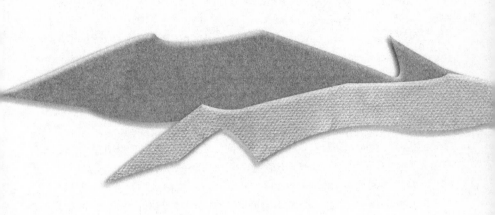

When the doors opened, it was the smell that hit you: almost sweet, but with the faint sour of turned flesh. More outsized fish—366 steelhead, to be precise, behemoth oceangoing trout—awaited me in a pair of cloud-white totes, voluminous and lined with translucent plastic bags. For a week, they had been thawing under the overhead heaters in the spawning house. Whenever the technicians needed to work inside, sorting or "collecting" the steelhead and salmon, they forklifted the totes into the March sunlight, aired out the place, hosed down the concrete floor. The flies enjoyed a taste, and then the fish were wheeled back in. But this was to be the last exit, for this batch. Soon more totes would be driven out of the freezer, where, for two weeks, the carcasses are kept at -10 degrees Fahrenheit to kill a parasite that will poison scavenging dogs.

I was drinking my coffee with Chuck Fustish, a salmonid biologist for the Oregon Department of Fish and Wildlife, having returned to the Cole Rivers Hatchery north of Medford. We had ridden upstream together to pick up the essential ingredient for tomorrow's "stream enrichment" session. With other volunteers, we were going to hurl these bad boys, these noxious remains, into one of the Rogue's nursery creeks. The idea was to simulate the natural die-off of salmon and steelhead, which no longer exists as it once did in the Northwest because of collapsed wild populations. These silver goliaths deliver not only thousands of eggs to their birth streams, but also all the sea-won nutrients in their rippling elephantine bodies. It is a crucial delivery, a key gift to river ecosystems, but in Oregon less than 10 percent of historic wild salmon and steelhead still exists. Surplus hatchery fish, however, we can toss. Over seventy thousand carcasses are launched into Oregon and Washington creeks each year.

The affable, and aptly named, Chuck wore a beige ODFW polo tucked into jeans below his stomach and a fluorescent orange ball cap that declared the agency's role in regulating the hunt. He has ice-blue eyes, curly gray hair, and a face genially askew to one side, his mouth sliding as if in a permanent Wyoming drawl. As a young man, Chuck gave up that sagebrush ocean for Oregon and his obsession with big fish, which he first glimpsed in the gloss of *National Geographic*. After earning a master's in fisheries at Oregon State, he migrated to the Rogue Valley, where he'd worked for ODFW for thirty-nine years. He would retire come June, in just a few months.

One of Chuck's diehard volunteers, Larry Butts, had ridden along as well, as he usually does the day before a carcass toss. Short and scrappy, with roseate thread veins in his pale cheeks, Larry had flown for the Navy and American Airlines before retiring to the Rogue Valley where he was raised. He was a fast but quiet talker, a fish zealot who drove a large green truck with a "Bend Over" anti-Obama sticker on the bumper.

Chuck, Larry, and company lob carcasses into the Rogue and its upper tributaries on ten Saturdays a year: salmon in the fall and early winter, steelhead in the spring, when each arrives. Salmon, "the king of fish," are famous for their all-or-nothing, one-and-done reproductive strategy, known as semelparity: After three or four years at sea, they run inland—potentially hundreds of miles—and devote every last ounce of their existence to broods of tangerine, oleaginous eggs buried loosely in gravel nests called "redds," which the females painstakingly excavate and groom with their tails. Then, without fail, they perish. Their carcasses sink away or float to nearby banks.

In fewer numbers, steelhead also go to the ocean, typically for two years, before returning inland; but the strongest among them, especially females, fin back to the Pacific once more, rejuvenate, and attempt the epic spawning journey all over again in future years: iteroparity. Genetically, steelhead are merely a rainbow trout, a grandiose maritime one, and scientists aren't sure why some trout fry become steelhead and others are content with freshwater. But probably this gigantism is genetic and an elaborate strategy, or anomaly, to bolster the species' fitness: It hedges bets against the vicissitudes of a single habitat; it hides roe in disparate baskets. In any case, for our modern enrichment purposes, a steelhead carcass serves just as well as a salmon's. Though a tad smaller and less iconic, it's an analogous sack of nutrients. It likewise stinks to high heaven. This spring alone Chuck and Larry would let fly eight tons of steelhead into Rogue tributaries.

The forklift whined in and out of the aseptic spawning house as it hoisted the totes onto Chuck's wooden flatbed trailer. It also loaded a third virginal tote between the laden, blood-spattered ones, just in case we needed to pitchfork some of the argentine bodies over to expose a frozen block below. "Otherwise," Larry told me, "you're sitting there with a crowbar and hammer trying to throw them into the stream. Tissue seems to hold its cold better than water." But these fish had left the freezer a week ago and it seemed turning the fish over, like the fertile compost they were, might not be necessary. As I stood by the totes, a playful breeze swirled and sent me reeling.

"Aren't they nice?" said Chuck. "You're going to love it."

"The smell takes some adjusting," I said.

"It gets better," Chuck replied.

Fading metallic, lightly freckled, the steelhead had settled into one another, each cradled in the soft valley of two more. Rather they had melted together: oozed, a mucilaginous film their temporary glue. On average each was four and a half pounds. Together they weighed sixteen hundred pounds. The genus of Pacific salmon and trout, *Oncorhyn-chus*, means "hook nose," and their jaws had grown long and sickled, becoming the "kypes" that display their fitness, their desirability. All, or nearly all, were male. At the hatchery, most females are squeezed of their sunset eggs with the push of a thumb and hauled downstream in a tanker truck to be "recycled," alive, back into the Rogue for anglers. But the males receive no such second chance, since they can't be stripped of their milt and so might spawn with wild fish, diluting the imperiled native gene pool if they "stray," if they don't return to the hatchery. Their only second chance is enrichment.

It was only males in jeans standing around these fish, I noticed—me, Chuck, Larry, and several hatchery employees. It was to be that kind of guys' weekend. We wended south toward Medford along the Crater Lake Highway, the Rogue gliding low and pitted beside us, bedrock visible in the river where it usually isn't: a dry year. I rode in the back of Chuck's cab, listening to Larry talk like a gentle riffle. Then onto a rolling back road through boutique wineries and old orchards, the famous Medford pear blossoms just emerged, pale and diaphanous, on their lumpish branches. Chuck prefers to avoid the main thoroughfares when towing fish so as not to create a public disturbance. "One time," said Chuck, "we let'm go real good, spring Chinook carcasses in the fall, and of course the flies are real thick at the end of the year. I had a trail of flies going from here to Medford. They were all trying to catch back up." No flies in our exhaust, so far as I could tell; the fish hadn't been thawed for long, and it wasn't yet the warm season. But our lone tailgater, a woman in a cream sedan, did pass us impatiently, and I wondered if it was Chuck's languid steering or if she'd caught a whiff.

∼‿⌢

We pulled into the Denman Wildlife Area, Chuck's headquarters, which rests in Central Point, adjacent to Medford, in the middle of the broad, fertile Rogue Valley. The unassuming office sat beside a tranquil pond with a view of snow-capped Mount McLoughlin, 9,495 feet in elevation, to the hazy east in the Cascades. It was a World War II army building turned faux chalet: forestry brown, with evergreen shutters sporting the cutout silhouettes of rising trout and antlered bucks. We rumbled past to a rear gravel lot and unhitched the trailer beside an aged red barn with dust holding the light in its cavernous mouth. The fish would benefit from an afternoon's sunbath.

Then we hit the highway, I-5, heading west a half hour to Grants Pass to drop off some little steelhead hitching a sloshy ride with us in a plastic trash can. Steelhead and salmon morph from newly hatched alevin to fry, to parr, to smolt, the stage when the fish silvers—ocean camouflage—and heads for salt. These were parr. At the hatchery, they had been netted from one of its concrete ponds for "an experiment." They were guinea pigs, canaries. They were going to be placed into a tiny creek, and if they survived, then ODFW would build a temporary barrier and pour in thousands more to "imprint" on the flow for several weeks. When the grown fish returned from the ocean, those survivors would rediscover their first stream—steelhead might be able to smell it from thirteen miles away—and linger, trying to find a way up despite an impassable dam. It was yet another ploy to bring luck to anglers.

To my surprise, we pulled into a skate park: That's what a nursery stream can look like these days. In flat-brimmed caps and baggy jeans sewn with graffiti letters, boys were swooping in and out of the smooth and sinuous dugout, a small concrete canyon, while across the lot a ditch ran between banks of mown grass: Skunk Creek. The water did look skunky, and most of this stretch was in full sun. But an incoming culvert dumped a froth in a shadowed pool, and maybe the fish would survive there.

As Chuck tentatively backed his truck toward the curb, Larry furtively slammed the butt of his fist against the door. It sounded as if we'd hit something, and we jumped. "Asshole," hooted Chuck, with nothing like true irritability. A local, salt-haired volunteer in rubber boots was waiting for us, a member of the Middle Rogue Steelheaders. He would coordinate feeding and monitoring the parr. Chuck dipped his green net into the trash can and turned it inside out, a perforated pocket, to count them as they tumbled like loose, living change into his palm. Ten, eleven . . . twelve. They had faint stripes on their sides like the shadows of new grass. He put them in a small wire-mesh trap, hinged, the shape of a barrel.

Larry and I looked on as Chuck sat on the tailgate to slide on hip-waders, and then he and the volunteer carefully climbed down the grassy slope to the pool half in shade. They were a little halting in their movements; they stepped circumspectly; and Larry confided in me then, "Another thing to worry about is that these volunteer groups are getting older, and younger people like yourself don't seem to be joining. I don't know if it's that they just don't care, or what." Maybe, I suggested, it wasn't apathy—though it well could be—but that youth are taking longer to home in, these days; that they are still in search of the places and things they loved.

We rubbernecked as Chuck tossed the barrel trap lightly into the water and tied it by a nylon cord to the bank. If these inconspicuous parr lasted in Skunk Creek, ODFW would open the valve of the tanker truck and pour in those shimmering thousands. Those little transplanted fish would grow into smolt and eventually the massive steelhead we'd left to rot in the sun in Central Point. "If the herons and boys don't get'm," said Chuck. If they survived the shallows and the deep.

We returned from Grants Pass through White City, the old World War II base turned industrial center of the Rogue Valley, which is surrounded by—intertwined with—nature reserves that harbor rare and endangered species like the large-flowered woolly meadowfoam and American pillwort. This savannah had been known as the Agate Desert and, in the patches of open space, you still can find not only semiprecious stones but also an endemic plant, the Agate Desert lomatium, found nowhere else. In 1942, Camp White was built on sixty-seven square miles and soon became known as "the Alcatraz of boot camps," because it was remote and tough. Replicas of German pillbox bunkers were, are, built into the side of Upper Table Rock, one of the prominent volcanic buttes on the north side of the Rogue Valley, and troops practiced storming them with live fire. After the camp was decommissioned, all but two square miles were sold as private real estate. But those two were handed over to ODFW for the common good.

Chuck stopped for government gas behind a warehouse in White City, and then, as we climbed back in the cab and drove the final stretch back to the wildlife area, he asked, "Did you hear the one about the biologists who went to hell?"

Larry and I had not.

"Well, the Devil said, 'Come on, boys, you got to choose.' And there were three doors. He opened the first door and there were people in fiiiire, burning up, and the biologists said, 'No, we don't want this.'

"So they went to the second door, and there were people in there, and they were gett'n tortured, torn apart and everything.

"Then they went to the third door, and there were all these guys standing up to their waists in old, dead Chinook carcasses, just drinking coffee. And they say, 'We'll take this one.' And the Devil says, 'Okay, get on in there n' get your coffee.'

"So they got in there with their coffee, and the Devil says, 'Okay, boys—coffee break is over. Down on your hands and knees.'"

At the wildlife area, we found the remainders of Friday's lunchtime barbeque. There was pepper-crusted salmon on the table with those no-see-um bones, thick and wet yellow potato salad, slim hot dogs, and Chuck's offering: a plastic tray of crackers, salami, and other round, sliced meat. "That's some good meat," Chuck observed, sampling as we ambled into the kitchen. "Here you go," he said, handing me a paper towel for a napkin. He pointed to the salmon in its foil nest and said, "I'll go halves with you." I forked six or seven lipidous mouthfuls into a New England–style hot dog bun and ate it as is, thinking about the long, fortuitous voyage this flesh had taken to my tongue.

The day's main chore accomplished, Chuck insisted I pocket some cookies for the road. "Ah, thanks," I said. "See you tomorrow morning for the toss." I drove out the refuge's gate and down the road through backyard orchards in anticipation of fitting in a hike up Lower Table

Rock, where ephemeral pools hold fairy shrimp and, as Larry told me, "you can dangle your feet right off the edge." But then I remembered: I'd meant to stay with the fish awhile, to honor them with a closer look before they disappeared tomorrow.

I U-turned, went back, parked, and walked unnoticed across the gravel lot to the red barn where the carcasses were basting in the raw light. The flies were waiting for me. A thousand iridescent, lapis backs lifted off annoyed, in a drone, but they quickly resettled, surmising I was an anemic threat. In the sun, the color of the fishes' bony gill plates had ripened to a peach-orange. Their skin had dried to a taut leather that showed their muscular weave beneath. Their mouths were uniformly agape and barred with teeth curved like fangs. Piled all together, they seemed a deposition of unending hunger.

Twenty minutes later, Chuck found me lurking with my black notebook. He sauntered across the gravel in his neon orange cap, a Coke sweating in hand as usual, to clean out his truck and ready it for tomorrow's enrichment. The fish were hitched and rearing to go nowhere.

"Couldn't get away, could you?" he said.

"Thought I'd muse on the fish awhile," I said.

The flies rose in a murmuring wreath as Chuck arrived and, after a pause, began to repopulate at a simmer. "Just think how deep we'd be buried in bodies if we didn't have flies," said Chuck. I wrote this down furiously.

Chuck then gave me an aerial tour of the fish, gross as they were. The bright peach-orange tint on their gill plates, the "operculum," is their breeding hue, he told me. Their teeth grow long and canine only while spawning: They aren't used for feeding, only for aggression or defense. The strange extra layers of teeth on their tongues are called "hyoid" teeth, but Chuck wasn't so sure about those on the roofs of their mouths, which looked like the sharp, conveyor-belt rows on the jaws of sharks. "Hey, I never took salmonid dentition," he said, drawing out the syllables. Steelhead feed to and from their freshwater rendezvous, but salmon don't feed at all, Chuck reminded me, not even a little, as they make their one and only pilgrimage inland. "If you take a migrating salmon and cut it open," he said, "it's chock-full of eggs or sperm, and its gut is like a thin ribbon."

"The thing that gets me most," Chuck said as he surveyed the awful landscape of the totes one last time and began to stroll toward his Prius, "is how a fish this big"—he spread his fingers a few inches, the size of one of the minnows that we'd dropped off at the skate park—"can go into the ocean, swim down to San Francisco, and return *this* big." He spread his hands beyond his shoulders.

It may be intuitive that a generous forest, a luxurious riparian buffer, benefits fish like salmon and steelhead. Trees are a stabilizing force. Salmonid embryos and fry are sensitive to temperature, and a lush, leaning canopy shades and cools the water, which lower on the Rogue can reach 80 degrees during the summer. Roots prevent erosion that can fill the interstices in redd gravel and choke the flow of oxygen and nutrients to buried eggs. Trees are also essential to rivers because they provide, and ultimately are, "large woody debris": which lodges and creates scouring pour-overs; which then become stable pools that protect spawning gravels during winter floods and allow fish to rest. The larger the debris, the longer it lasts and the less likely it is to be swept off. In rivers thirty feet wide, generally only trunks a foot and a half in diameter withstand the most intimidating flows. Additionally leaf litter is fodder for aquatic insects that juvenile fish devour. Thus, along with overfishing, dams, and now climate change, the legacy of logging is a major reason salmonid populations have plummeted so sharply in the Northwest.

But what if salmon and steelhead are also critical to forest health? They are, we've found, and the reason is simple: Their bodies are tidy packages of nitrogen from the ocean, packages that dissolve. Typically nitrogen—a component of both the chlorophyll used in photosynthesis and the nucleic acids found at the heart of every cell—is the limiting factor for vegetative growth in Northwest forests. Not much is available to organisms on land, but plenty dissolves from the air into the ocean, where it is transformed or "fixed" by certain microbes, turning into ammonium that other microorganisms can readily access and incorporate into their bodies. As a result, the ocean is fertile while the freshwater and terrestrial ecosystems are, in many places, "nutrient-poor." Fortunately more than 95 percent of a salmon's palatial bulk accrues in the ocean, where they feast on krill swarms that lend their supple flesh its orange-pink. Each returning fish embodies about sixty-five grams of nitrogen.

Scientists have shown that steelhead and salmon swim up into the trees, so to speak—especially salmon, because they are so well studied. The key to this discovery is isotopes: two or more forms of an element that have the same number of protons (which is essential to the atom's chemical identity), but differing numbers of neutrons. A nitrogen atom usually has fourteen neutrons, but less commonly it can grab one more. About 12 percent of the nitrogen in the sea happens to be of this rarer fifteen-neutron variety, while on the continent there is pretty much none.

Along streams, even far inland, researchers have collected foliage samples and ground them to a fine powder for spectrometer analysis, which allows us to pinpoint the isotopic ratio. An elevated N-15 to N-14 ratio signals a contribution from the ocean. In reaches where salmon spawn and die, up to a third of the nitrogen found in leaves is marine-born, the gift of carcasses. Core samples from these trees, which allow us to compare annual growth rings, show that the growth rate along these enriched streams is as much as triple and an increase is significant as far as three hundred feet from the bank. Which means, at healthy spawning sites—at funerary sites—it might take less than a hundred years for a tree to reach that flood-resistant girth of a foot and half, when it would take three hundred years otherwise. In this way, anadromous ("up-running") fish are crucial for the vigor and recovery of forests and streams. They generate shade and debris that, in turn, support their own reproduction. And of course, the taller the trees, the farther away from the bank they can topple and still make a splash.

It's a classic, exemplary ecological cycle, but this positive-feedback loop is terribly frayed throughout the Northwest. Only a fraction of the "nutrient subsidy" that anadromous fish once offered river ecosystems is still delivered. In extreme cases, up to 95 percent of the nitrogen and phosphorous in watersheds once came from salmon, and their infusion of carbon also invigorated the food web. But Pacific salmon are now found in only 40 percent of their natural range and, within those waterways, they deliver just 7 percent of the nutrients of old. In the

Snake River Plain of Idaho, notoriously beleaguered by dams, a paltry 2 percent of historic salmon numbers have arrived in the past forty years.

In more ways than one, then, the strength of the run dictates the number of smolts that later will travel out to sea. Fewer parents mean fewer eggs, obviously; but fewer carcasses also mean the "carrying capacity" of the river gradually falls and, for lack of food and shelter, fewer juveniles will be able to survive down the line. In essence, the riverbank is overdrawn. You have a "net nutrient export": Smolts go to sea, but adults don't return. As a result, many conservation efforts are at risk of sabotage. A stretch of pristine or restored river might look like paradisiacal salmon and steelhead country, but if adult fish aren't already running strong, it's probably malnourished. Wild rivers can't rely on the massive bags of fish feed that arrive on pallets at hatcheries like Cole Rivers, however. Or they could, but there's a more holistic, if not transcendent, way to fertilize, to jump-start the "riverweb": one carcass at a time. In the words of Chuck, "Gives the whole system a shot in the arm."

There were glazed donuts in the morning, and a waiver. Larry was there, along with two other volunteers, Steve Brummett and Tom Treese, both retirees. Steve was a lanky California figure with white hair to his shoulders, glasses, and severe cheek lines. He wore a baby blue UCLA cap, the gold of its Bruins *B* exactly matching his down Patagonia vest. Tom's suspenders held up black rain pants. He had a full face, a trim gray mustache, and an ODFW volunteer cap—one of the perks of this filthy job. He'd moved to Medford from San Diego where he'd run a construction scaffold business, and he liked to remind us that he was born in Oregon, though he left as a baby. These guys squeezed into the cab of Chuck's four-by-four with me, while Larry wheeled off separately to pick up the last member of the crew and endeavor to beat us to the toss site.

We took the Lake of the Woods Highway east toward the Cascades, past muddy ATV tracks and broken cars abandoned in fields. The white cone of Mount McLoughlin grew until it finally sunk behind the green foothills we drove into. Earlier known as Snowy Butte, this stratovolcano had lent its name to Little Butte Creek, which soon we sailed across at fifty miles per hour. The size of a one-lane road, Little Butte ran swift and opaque with silt; seventeen miles east to west, it empties into the Rogue across from Upper Table Rock. "Don't let me miss the turn," said Chuck. "It's Lake Creek Road."

No flies trailed us into Lake Creek, so named for a branch of the Little Butte: There are tributaries upon tributaries for fish to swim up and call home. The town was only a grange as white as a chapel, a log-cabin pioneer hall, a general store, and a handful of houses. Just beyond, we turned left up the South Fork of the Little Butte and followed it through ranchland studded with petite black oak, wiry and handsome. Past a turn for Dead Indian Road, the pass over the hills to Ashland, the valley began to narrow and evergreen. Then up ahead was a temporary *Caution* sign, an orange diamond. Chuck slowed and steered us around a rockslide in the middle of the gravel road. Amid the rubble was the tawny medusa of an uprooted madrone tree.

"Quite the fall down here," said Tom. "Goodness gracious."

"That's a good one," said Chuck.

"Damn," said Steve.

"Don't let Marian see all those rocks," said Tom. "She'd have me over here trying to get some for the garden."

We came to the end of the line, a concrete bridge with its piers buttressed by heavy riprap. Chuck drove the rig on and over and performed a careful three-point turn. "Come on back, come on back," said Tom, waving into the side mirror. "There you go, looking good." Obscure in the hemlock was Camp Latgawa, a Methodist retreat you can rent for your next gathering outside of Medford. "The end of the canyon," reads its brochure. "The beginning of a journey." In the language of the Rogue Valley's Natives, *Latgawa* means "those living in the uplands." The Takelma people wintered along these tributaries, relying on steelhead and salmon, and in the summer they climbed the ridges to hunt deer, gather huckleberries, and escape the infernal heat.

Mid-bridge, Chuck cut the engine. "All right," he said, "we're ready." Larry and John Thiebes, a retired ODFW biologist and our final tosser, had caught up and eaten our plume of dust, and now, without ceremony, everyone snapped on latex gloves the hue of clear skies. They hoisted the fish pughs—short poles with sharp, gently hooked tips—from Chuck's pickup bed and began to spear the long-marinated carcasses, one at a jab. They carried them dripping along the bridge, planted their feet, and flung the poles forward like lacrosse sticks. The fish twirled heavily outward, flashing and spraying, and crashing through the willow to another existence.

Chuck played foreman and supervised as the steelhead were skewered and sent packing. "John has got four on the bank so far," he said, with a guffaw. The idea was to throw them into the water, where, in theory, they would have once died naturally.

"What!" said John. In his jostling green waders, he scampered to the bridge's edge and peered down through dark sporty sunglasses, a tarnished fish swaying from his pugh. As a former regional coordinator for ODFW biologists, until recently John had been Chuck's boss; Chuck told me that the acronym for John's official title had turned out to be PRIM DIC, in all seriousness. But he was a really nice guy.

"Oh, shoot," John said, dumping his steelhead over the side. "I didn't even notice that, Chuck. I didn't see that the creek went around an island." The water's flow was subdued this year as the drought in the West deepened.

"That's all right," Chuck said. "There's crittters that'll eat'm."

"Ooo, doubleheader," said Steve, lifting two fish on his pugh, each grinning and dripping devilishly.

"Ooo, here's one with maggots on it," said John. They squirmed like extra teeth in the steelhead's mouth.

The scene was the inverse of an old fishing site, I imagined, where Natives and settlers alike would have lanced or netted salmon and steelhead from rocks at falls. It was tradition played in reverse, a renewal, a repentance for past sins: the ruination of spine-tingling fish runs. As the steelhead were ushered along the bridge, the morning light shone amber through the triangles of their flimsy tails. Sometimes the guys just shook them off directly into the creek. Sometimes they flung with all their might. Steve stood on the trailer's platform and chucked, slow and steady. He stared each steelhead in the eye, holding it aloft; then he watched its body sink or roll away like a man contemplating his golf shot.

John Thiebes explained to me why they tossed them instead of simply dumping the whole lot. "There are so many little different currents in a creek," he said. "The more varied you put them in, the more highly distributed they'll be." In other words, the proverbial butterfly effect comes into play: The slightest difference in where a carcass lands could mean a wild difference in its final resting place; could mean miles of drifting or whether a bruin scatters it through the woods to feed the trees. Tossed carcasses are known to wander several feet, to a few miles, to, in one recorded case, twelve miles downstream.

Chuck then handed me a clean pugh and I speared one through its rancid shine and lifted it from the half-frozen, sticky mass. Walking to the railing, I loaded the ponderous fish, its surprising weight, over my shoulder. Its jaws hung open as if in anticipation. It gave no objection. Awkwardly, it catapulted, remembering nothing of its fluidness, except for the fetid arc of ruby droplets that may or may not have decorated me.

Upon impact—*smack*—the leakage must have been explosive. Finally the river began to consume this steelhead, to reclaim its contents. A carcass acts as a "slow-release" fertilizer and, after a month submerged, will lose more than 40 percent of its mass, deflating like a bladder. Nymphs would crawl across its skin; a fungus shag would eventually coat it. Within a hundred feet downstream, a bumper crop of "biofilm"—a slick matrix of algae and bacteria—would thrive on underwater rocks and fuel grazing insects. Aquatic invertebrates might increase eightfold, temporarily. Meanwhile, the willows, fir, and hemlock along Little Butte would absorb their share of downwelling nitrogen and invest it preferentially, not in root development or foliar maintenance, but in tender furnaces, new shoots and leaves. Leaves that would eventually twirl and drown.

"All aboard!" Chuck shouted, calling us off the bridge. We slid the pughs into the pickup's bed and hopped onto the trailer. Ruefully, I gripped the juicy rim of a tote as we rattled downstream to a second, and then a third, tossing spot, both with an easy window through the willow to the creek. Midway through the morning, the bins turned a little soupy. The remaining fish sunk into a slush the not-so-vibrant color of uncooked steak past its prime. John dedicated himself to prying the bottommost dwellers loose from this icy slurry of blood and ooze with his gloved hands. Like a monger, he tossed the fish underhand onto the grassy shoulder between the road and river, where they bounced and skidded, and waited for us to stab and project them into the Little Butte.

Now you had to be careful where you stood: John kept us on our toes. Was he aiming for our feet? He was. One toss grazed my sneaker, and I knew my laces would waft for days. From a long way off, John then managed to torpedo Larry while he wasn't looking. "Asshole," said Larry with reluctant admiration. Luckily he was wearing a Gore-Tex jacket. Karma kicked in, eventually, when John's hat fell into a tote. "Shoot," he muttered, whisking it up. "Shoot" was an understatement. He studied his cap, and put it back onto his balding head though it was damp with mucous and serum. "That's okay," he reassured himself. "It's my fishing hat." But flies would orbit him later.

I found myself standing by Steve as the totes were drawn down. Each time his pugh punctured the loose bag of a fish, a pop was heard, a dismal sound. When he cast, he let go of the pugh with his trailing right hand and let the pole drift outward in his left with the fish's momentum, just as you might cast a fishing rod. After a time, his tosses barely reached the creek. Twice in a row, his steelhead smacked off a dry boulder and deflected into the water.

"Bank shot," said Steve. "I think I'm getting tired."

The valleys of his cheeks seemed to deepen, to stretch into a grimace, with each toss. He began to wobble slightly; his follow-through carried him out of kilter so that he'd have to take a step or two. I imagined a heavy door might throw him off balance sometimes, as it does for me. We are both tall and willowy. Even as dead weight, these fish reminded us of their muscle and ours, and it was hard to say who was denser.

"I'm looking tired," said Steve, as if seeing himself through our eyes. Stooped in the shoulders, drained. Under his gold vest, he was, in fact, a relatively slight man.

"I think you need a break," Chuck said, stepping forward as foreman.

"I need a break," Steve agreed.

Chuck took Steve's pugh and hurled until, before long, the steelhead were gone and all that remained on the bank were dark stains on the soil and the frozen embers of roe scattered in the grass. Turns out, a few of the fish had been female. At the hatchery, they'd drawn a short stick and been offered no second chance. Or maybe this was theirs. I imagined that yellow jackets would find these pellucid orange delicacies and wing them off, glowing, like tiny rogue suns.

As Chuck gunned down the gravel with the lightened trailer swaying and clanging behind us, from the back seat I asked him and Tom what there was to be said, in the end, about the art of tossing carcass. We were headed back to the Cole Rivers Hatchery at Lost Creek Lake to get rid of the slimy totes.

"How about being damn good exercise," said Tom.

"A strong back and a weak nose," replied Chuck. "That's what you need."

"How about a strong back and a weak mind," said Tom.

"That too," said Chuck.

We took a back road along the Little Butte to its intersection with Crater Lake Highway, in the town of Eagle Point. The creek swelled to the size of a river as it slid past neat ranches with hay and RVs under open-air barns. Tom pointed out where he and Chuck had planted seedling pines or pumped farm ponds dry to kill invasive snails. He remembered his first carcass toss with Chuck, up another tributary of the Rogue, Elk Creek. That was seven years ago. The snow had been deep, unlike this spring. They talked of the guys who had helped them heave; they talked of those men's wives.

"I saw Madonna the other day," said Tom, who always spoke as if trying to catch his breath. "Went to that memorial for Linda Wood."

Chuck nodded and said, "I thought that was pretty cool that they dumped her ashes right where they dumped his."

"Yeah," said Tom. "Jeff. Miss them both. Their daughters were real nice, very receptive. They called us that morning. She died at something like two thirty in the morning, and I think by seven thirty the phone rang. It was Dina? Dina or Diane. Anyway, one of the daughters called and let us know that Linda had passed. Such a sweet lady . . . God, I enjoyed fishing with Jeff. He was just so nice. Wonderful guy."

In Eagle Point, we rumbled past the historic Butte Creek Mill, founded in 1872, early for Oregon. It's the oldest gristmill in existence west of the Mississippi, and the only one still active in the Beaver State. Stones from France were carted by wagon from Crescent City on the California coast, and afterward farmers throughout the region carted their wheat to Eagle Point. The mill took every seventh bag as payment, selling it in their general store and trading it to the Klamath tribe—the local Takelma had been run out of the territory already—for hide and dried berries.

Until the mid-nineties there was no fish screen on the mill's tailrace, so those migrating salmon and steelhead that chose this dark passage, instead of going over the dam, were minced in the turbine like grain under the stone one floor above. In the basement, a rusted pitchfork now leans against the wall to show visitors how the mill owners once speared their main course from the flume. But today a dedicated fish conduit exists and, for a while, ODFW counted the fish that passed through. In 2002, twenty-five thousand steelhead fry—and over 6.5 million spring Chinook salmon fry—traveled downstream. It was a drought year, like this one, and more fish had been forced to spawn in the Rogue's larger creeks such as Little Butte.

We passed a chic school that Chuck visited each year, one of twenty-five, to talk salmon and give each classroom five hundred Chinook eggs to raise in an aerated aquarium. "You go in there," said Chuck, with wonder, "and there's no blackboard—they're all sitting in front of computers." Barring disaster, the kids eventually release their minnow salmon into a local stream. Thus the Rogue Valley's youth learn and hopefully begin to care about their native fish and watershed. Begin to home in. Each teacher is asked to eventually turn in a report noting how many salmon they pour into the neighborhood. The state wants even that data, though from ten thousand eggs, the whole program, only three adults are likely to return. This year, Chuck's last, was the first time that every teacher had submitted a report to him. "One of the biologists up in Salem," Chuck recalled, "she used to send out a Certificate of Death if you didn't send in your end-of-the-year report. Oh, they didn't like that."

I asked Chuck why he was retiring just now, as if the answer weren't plain. "Cause I'm eligible," said Chuck, gazing at me with his glacial eyes through the rearview mirror, "and I'm seeing myself not getting the time to do the things I want to do, like go fishing and hunting, and traveling in my trailer. It's always work, work, work, and every night, when I go home from work, I'm so damn tired I just fall asleep." He talked of revisiting the alpine lakes he had fished in Wyoming as a boy.

"Don't you get over there and retire and then turn around and die on us," said Tom, "or I'll come over and piss on your grave."

"No, no, no," said Chuck.

"I won't stand for that shit," Tom said.

"No, I ain't going to die, that's for sure."

We listened to the purr of the truck, the rattle of the dash.

"It's about time you're able to go and do what you want to do," said Tom.

"Thirty-nine years is enough," Chuck agreed. "The body is starting to de-te-ri-o-rate." He isolated each syllable.

At the hatchery, we pulled up to an empty navy-blue dumpster. Tom and Chuck slid on four more disposable gloves and, between them, hoisted the clear bags that lined the totes. Some of the bloody liquid, sloshing within, spritzed from where the pughs had punctured the film. Then we drove the totes a hundred yards to the spawning house, coming full circle. Under an overhead nozzle, we wrestled the hollow bins off the trailer. Chuck yanked on a wall-mounted lever to release a stream from above into each tote, frothing the syrupy remainder to the blush of a rosé. This way it wouldn't dry before the hatchery employees returned on Monday. They would rinse the totes, sterilize them, and stack them along the chain-link until it was time to "collect" again, to freeze and thaw and haul up another tributary. On the way out, Tom and I each ate a glazed donut in triumph, but Chuck declined, said he wasn't hungry.

As the sun began to draw the shadows of the elfin black oaks across the wintergreen ranches, I drove back up Little Butte Creek to stay with the fish once more. The carcass toss had been a whirlwind; the fish had burdened the pughs and our nostrils for no more than an hour. Now the real work would begin, the long decomposition. Chuck had told me that, in cold water, a carcass might last four to eight weeks, though in warmer cases a week would suffice for its disappearance. Each fish, he said, would soon have a crawdad looking out from its open maw. "They eat their way out," Steve had added. I wanted to spend more time with the fish, to see where they had first settled and stand by.

Past the immaculate grange, I stopped at the Lake Creek General Store and found, on the bathroom wall, a kitschy metal sign that read, *I say we fish five days a week and work two*, beneath the silhouette of a man and his boy, the generations, sitting side-by-side in ten-gallon hats with their rods. I bought a black coffee to go that I planned to save and curved lazily up the South Fork again under the basalt buttes as the valley began to funnel and fill with conifer and shadow. Pairs of Canada geese loitered in the fecund pastures. A Holstein cow rested its head lightly on the rump of another.

When I stepped from the car at the site of the morning's final toss, the smell, an old friend by now, rose up to greet me. It had soaked into the ground where John Thiebes had tossed the fish at our boots and made us dance. It clung to the thin grass newly between the gravel and was embodied in the orange roe that now caught my eye like polished sea glass. From the road's shoulder, I could see the steelhead where they'd come to rest below in the stream: ghost white, cuticles in the river. The cold had forced the rouge from their skin and carried it inside or away.

Down the bank, I stepped, to study three steelhead jammed like logs behind a boulder. I was pretty sure one of them was a fish I had tossed, one that had barely reached the Little Butte. Pinned by the current, they seemed frozen in an association they might have known in another life: Some moment of spawning, maybe. Some flurry of defense or fondness. The kype of one male was raised above water, barely, and its golden eye flickered in the clear pulse that rolled up its face. The fin of its neighbor was also lifted into the air and quivering like a tuning fork. Nearby, another fish hung broken in a willow, flies resting on the red jamb of its lip. An accidental sky burial.

Past the *Caution* sign and the rockslide, I arrived at the bridge to Camp Latgawa. Some of the steelhead here, the first we'd thrown, had washed a few hundred feet downstream. Descending the bank through blackberry and willow, I waded into the stream in my rubber boots and was absorbed by the noisy silence of the creek. The fish were wrapped around stones like wrecks around telephone poles. I nudged a few over with my toe and looked into their sodden mouths for crawdads, but none had arrived. Not yet. Their eyes bulged opal white. Two pale fish were snagged in the woody debris on either side of a riffle, just where the creek fell into waves; these reminded me of marble statues guarding an edifice, a library, all of it submerged and overturned.

Carcasses can be held by large and small boulders, slow margin-water, and pocket-pools; they can be buried by gravel quickly or over time, abandoned above the waterline by receding flows, or held in the tentative grips of roots, the washboards of riffles, and living branches. Scavengers wrestle them onto the banks and scatter them for others. But it's a complex logjam, intricately woven with sticks and branches, that is the best retainer of the dead. Trees are the original, unwitting fishers, stringing seines across creeks to drag for salmon and steelhead and, in the long run, nurture more of them. Or maybe it's the fish that are unknowingly raising and culling the trees.

Then, in a half-dry channel below the bridge, lay a fish at rest in a shallow puddle. Half-exposed to the air, lending its oil to the pool's surface—evidence that it already had begun to leach, to pass on. And there on its side were three gray moths, adhered, each pasted upside down to the fish's scales. To a moth, it was clear, a steelhead carcass can be a fatal moon. They had visited in the dusk and become stuck to its mucal surface.

But bending lower, I saw: They were still alive. The legs of one moth tickled the air, and when a second managed to raise a wing in instinct or memory of flight, its upper surface showed violet-blue. These weren't moths, I realized: They were those small blue butterflies so fond of roads and trails, the genus *Celastrina*; those spring azures, as they're known, that "mud-puddle" in clusters, especially the males, to drink the sodium they require to breed; fragile two-fold creatures that advertise the sky, but, when they close their wings, are perfectly camouflaged on gravel or in the salty ash of a campfire.

〜〜〜

I slept diagonally in back of the Jeep, in the sleeping bag I had stolen from my father long ago, ancient and baby blue, with the down half-gone out of its cells. My breath gradually fogged the windows as the night cooled and locked me in. We were in the mountains, I realized, we were near headwaters. Sometime in the early morning dark, I pushed open a rear door to piss and shiver. The quarter-moon poured down and the fish shone chalk white in the Little Butte like stones for someone to cross. But not me.

Direct sun on Little Butte around nine. The fish hadn't budged, not that I could see. No bear in the night, no raccoon. I drove a quarter mile upstream past the rockslide to Camp Latgawa and walked the concrete bridge again, eating a banana and drinking my frigid day-old coffee in the building sun. The willows were lit with the nibs of their new buds. The stream continuously divided around the elliptical island of cobbles where John Thiebes's errant steelhead still lay stranded. Other carcasses were also mostly as they had been the day before: bandaged around stones, their opercula pried open like doors by the current, their pale bellies an invitation.

Even from high on the bridge, the flies were now visible. There were at least fifty on the burnished flank of the steelhead that, last night, had trapped the spring azures. I scrambled down the purple slate riprap and, as I came upon that particular fish, my shadow seemed to become the flies it raised to nearby rocks. The three butterflies were still there, held in the wetness, clinging to the body. As I knelt in the mud to photograph them in the morning light, one lifted a wing and revealed its lavender-blue. They had survived the chilly night with their backs, their microscopic scales, glued to the fish's.

The flies' confidence returned and so did they, at a trickle. One twitched to an overturned butterfly and with rubbing forelegs prodded its fellow insect. Their legs engaged, bicycled in concert. Some transpiration: our beauty and our hideousness communing, though, this close, they were difficult to tell or tease apart. They were one animal. The lustrous flies gathered faster and nosed into the openings—the gill slit, the quarter-inch wound at the base of the pectoral fin—where they turned to oviposit. This is how the fish would begin to disseminate, one larva-cum-fly at a time. Fifty thousand maggots, I've read, will grow in a salmon carcass and devour it completely within five days.

A salmonid carcass is an environment unto itself, an ephemeral eco-system. More than sixty species of insect from thirty-six families were found teeming on carcasses marooned in British Columbia, especially saprophagous ("putrid-eating") flies. These in turn lure tiny predators. Certain parasitic wasps carry high concentrations of marine nitrogen, because their larvae feast on fly larvae raised on salmon. In fact, chemically speaking these wasps are as much of the ocean as sea lions or orca whales: They're on the same trophic level, the same step of the pyramid. Slugs and snails slime across carcasses; ants, beetles, spiders, bristletails, cave crickets, mites, and springtails arrive opportunistically. And in the footprint, "the hotspot," of a dead fish there is heightened subterranean burrowing: Millipedes and worms thrive in the enriched soil. So do roots.

How much nitrogen does a dying fly then bequeath to the earth or to the bird, the viridescent tree swallow, that catches it? The answer doesn't matter to me, ultimately. Just the fact of it. The act of it. The face. A fly will have a nitrogen "signature" specific to the fish in which it was born.

Back on the bridge, waiting for some further sign, I spotted a mink—a shaggy, brown member of the weasel family, an aquatic specialist and nemesis of crawdads. It galumphed swiftly up the rocks with obsidian eyes, and once more I held my breath. Surely it would find and scavenge one of these fish. On some rivers, more than 40 percent of carcasses are strewn inland as scraps or scat. Chuck had seen bald eagles descend on the freshly tossed. "Bears get a hold of them," he also told me, "and you know what happens when you get'm: They tear'm up and run'm through. That spreads them to the far reaches of the riparian area." Where the run is strong, bears eat the brains, eggs, and dorsal muscles, and leave the dregs to the smaller world. The trees get the bear shit, too.

This mink was no bear, though, and it kept bounding, under me and the concrete span, and upstream through the glowing lattice of living and dead willow. It would find the carrion later, or maybe it had already had its fill. It wasn't alive to fulfill my story. Instead, I found my banana peel where I'd accidentally left it, draped on the wood rail of the bridge. In an hour of sun, its skin had mottled entirely black and brown.

But this journey will finish as you might expect: They did come, at precisely eleven thirty on a Sunday morning, just as I first felt the wind touch my face. Or perhaps I noticed the warming breeze only after those three drifted nonchalantly overhead, from behind, on rigid up-tilt wings of silver primaries. But I don't think so; the wind and the hoodless birds arrived as one. The pink of their low, passing faces reminded me of the alpenglow that burns on the cheek of a spawning steelhead.

They triangulated in the V-shaped canyon, trolling stiffly across the spires of conifer, circling the few hundred meters to which the fish had been randomly delivered. So many bodies confused them, I thought, made it more difficult to home in. They didn't land as I watched, but they would. They would defecate steelhead onto their feet, as vultures do to keep them free of bacteria. They would carry these fish—this ocean—to their basalt cliffs, to their downy white nestlings hissing in some concealed recess.

It was then that I felt I could end my vigilance and let the fish live.

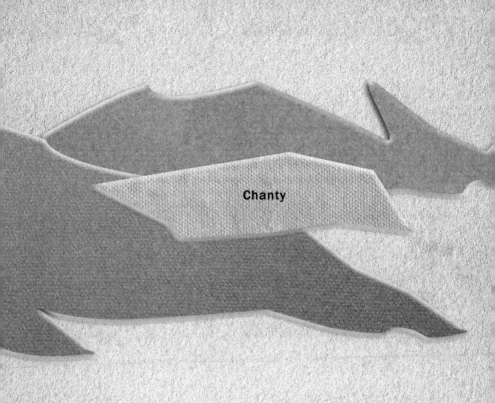
Chanty

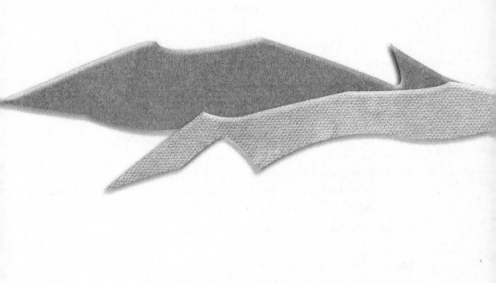

Lift this cup and drink the scent of apricot and mud.

Of wet California winters in the rambling woodlands: red-berried toyon and blue hound's tongue, madrone and bay laurel, oak and poison oak.

Cut through, the flesh is firm and white, the aroma also slightly peppery.

In profile, a fresh slice of chanterelle might remind of a horned skull, bleached in the desert, in a rain shadow, far from its natural clime.

Or Georgia O'Keeffe's flowers: those intimate lines and pastels, which suggest unfolding. A mushroom is also a fruiting body.

Most often, mushrooms are likened to male anatomy. Perhaps the chanterelle, more elegant and freeform, suggests the limits of metaphor.

That a chanterelle is a chanterelle is a chanterelle is a chanterelle.

No: It invites metaphor, and they multiply. As if by spore.

The ancient Greeks made a wide, footed drinking vessel, the *kantharos*, with looping handles that rise above its lip; on the vessel's side, human figures were often painted in black and orange, as if in procession around its curve.

Helmeted warriors with ornate shields and drawn swords; women in robes, pearls in their ears; pipers and harpists.

Above the lips, I mean. Meant to be held with two hands, carefully. Fired at a thousand degrees, thousands of years ago.

Many, many more.

Chanterelle, the French diminutive: little cup.

They're found on every continent except Antarctica. More than ninety species, several of which exist on multiple continents.

Anzutake, in Japan: apricot mushroom. *Pfifferling*, in Germany: little pepper. In the Valle de México, the Nahuatl say *xochilnanácatl*: flower mushroom.

~~~

The nude sporocarp, of course, is only temporary, an offering of the buried organism, the near-invisible mycelium running through the soil with filaments known as hyphae.

From the Greek *huphe*, "web."

In the case of chanterelle, these fibrils entwine with the roots of a nearby tree, diligently feeding it nitrogen and phosphorous in exchange for a modest drink of sugar, born of sun.

Thus their golden color, I imagine.

Hexoses, which the fungus transmutes into mannitols, arabitols, and erythritols.

This symbiosis is known as "mycorrhiza": "root," "of fungus." We have discovered that the vast majority of the world's plant species find such a coupling essential.

Stoop to a chanterelle and, as your fingers touch its flesh, you touch the crown of the tree casting the shade in which you stand.

But what if all words are symbiotic.

"Metaphor," for example: *meta*-, "with, across, or after"; and *phor*, "to carry, bear."

Consider that, if one utters "chanterelle," one reaches not only to *kantharos*, but further to the Greek *kanthus*, for "side," "edge," "border."

"Decant": to pour over a rim, slowly.

From *kanto*, from *kamb-to*, from the proto-Indo-European root *Kemb-*: to bend, turn.

Just so, the potter shapes his clay.

A hypha is a single cell thick, allowing it to absorb nutrients from whatever it worms through or around. It grows from the tip: As water is absorbed, pressure increases within the cell until it bulges forward, and a wall develops behind, pinching off another link.

"Hyphen," from the Greek *huphen*, "together": *hupo*, "under," and *hen*, "one."

Before long, the sheath or mantle of mycorrhizal hyphae wraps around a hair of a root so that, through an electron microscope, together they look like twine around a spindle.

Zoom in, once more: The hyphae nose between the root's epidermal cells, pushing into their crevices, forming what's called "the Hartig net," the interface for exchange.

From the proto-Indo-European *Kemb-* came the Celtic *kamb-i-*, which became the Latin *cambiāre*. Change, as they say, is inevitable.

And cambium, the living tissue that rings the dead heartwood of a tree, the xylem and phloem that feeds and is fed by the chanterelle buried below.

From a single spore, a "mycelium mat," that hidden tangle of hyphae, can grow to be acres in size, uniting and nursing multiple trees. Even those of different species. It creates a network of nutrient and chemical flow that reduces the risk of all, balancing the forest.

Communicating, some would argue.

Theories for the *urheimat*, the origin of Indo-European language:

That the root lies on the Pontic-Caspian steppe, north of the Black Sea, where the horse was first domesticated; where, between 4,000 and

3,000 B.C., the Kurgan nomads, a cluster of warring cultures, spread across Europe and the Near East carrying the mother tongue.

The German *mutter*, the Russian *mat*, the Persian *madar*, the Polish *matka*, the Sanskrit *mata*, the Latin *mater*.

Or that our language began to travel earlier between 7,000 and 6,000 B.C. from Anatolia, now Turkey, where cereals were domesticated and agriculture arose. In turn, growing populations radiated outward, mixing with others and supplanting their languages.

That God looked down and saw a rising tower: "Behold, the people *is* one, and they have all one language; and this they begin to do: and now nothing will be restrained from them, which they have imagined to do."

From the base of an oak, a chanterelle mycelium may develop and spread below ground for decades, unnoticed and uncollected. Never once mushrooming. Then it may fruit perennially, for centuries. Just so long as the tree stands.

The largest living organism in the world is thought to be a parasitic honey mushroom mycelium, *Armillaria solidipes*, in eastern Oregon. It's estimated that, for over two thousand years, the mushroom has spread beneath two thousand acres. It was discovered from an airplane because, in this case, the nutrients flow only one way, killing the pine forest and so forming a giant footprint on the land.

Luckily, the chanterelle cooperates.

Below the surface, the mycelium of a fungus gathers into primordia, nodules of woven hyphae less than two millimeters in diameter. They begin to swell and push upward.

An incipient ziggurat, a shrine to reach the foggy heaven; one destined to disintegrate, to become gelatin, in three or four weeks' time.

~~~~

"Go to," He said, "let us go down, and there confound their language, that they may not understand one another's speech."

"Babel," from the Hebrew *balal*, "to jumble." *Ba* and *ma*, the exclamations of a baby.

Yet the original Indo-European lexicon includes words for "wheel," "axle," "harness-pole," and "to go or convey in a vehicle," which suggests these inventions already existed, that our cognates rode into the present on conquering chariots: the Kurgans.

That every single word, after all, is a metaphor, carrying us across time.

Kantarel, kantarell, kanterlla, kantarelli: Dutch, Swedish, Icelandic, Finnish.

They begin as buttons. They bloom into a sprawling canopy of waving edges that sometimes lifts a handful of forest humus on its cratered back: a floating island planted with an oak seedling, maybe, or even a few worms.

"When you take a flower in your hand and really look at it," said O'Keeffe, "it's your world for a moment."

"Mud puppies," some pickers say. A vase isn't necessarily meant to hold flowers.

Of course, the metaphor of a tree is often used to describe the dissemination of speech, each node of the past branching toward increasing complexity, as if seamlessly.

The main limbs: Celtic and Germanic. Italic, Balto-Slavic, and Balkan. Hellenic, Armenian, Indo-Iranian.

~⌐~

(Anatolian and Tocharian, now extinct.)

Each word like a stoma on a leaf, opening and closing. All our "material" stemming from the Latin *materia*: tree trunk.

But maybe a mycelium is the stronger metaphor, since language is more fluid or labyrinthian, traveling in waves, back and forth and often underground, across centuries and cultures. Evolving in the very act of speech and, now, writing.

Where winters are cold in North America, the chanterelle climbs out of the earth at the return or height of summer. But along the more temperate Pacific Coast, the first chanterelle appears two weeks after a cold December rain.

Cantharellus formosus, the golden mushroom I know from the Northwest. The Latin *formosus*: beautiful, handsome; aesthetic, well-formed.

Close cousin to the eastern North American and European species, *cibarius*: edible.

Go forth on Christmas morning. Go ahead. Wear old shoes. Carry a wicker basket, or a paper grocery bag folded in your back pocket.

An optimistic heart.

A hollow at the base of a shady, north-facing amphitheater: a bowl in the hillside with a downed tree and bramble winding across the ground.

Smell of bay leaf.

~⌐~

Even from a distance, chanterelles seem to call out to a beginner, one of the easiest mushrooms to see in the woods, to stumble across. Always inviting my attention.

Catching the corner of the eye: the "canthus," where the lids meet and tears gather to drop over an edge, to slide down a cheek; a word which means just as it did in ancient Greece.

And the neighboring proto-Indo-European root, *Kand-*: to shine. Candle. Incandescence. Candidate, from *candidatus*, "white-robed," the purity of the toga.

The candid flesh, the incendiary pan. The white chanterelle, *Canthar-ellus subalbidus*, which is ever partial to Douglas fir.

There are many foragers who hunt only chanterelle, for they are abundant, choice, and not easily confused for the poisonous, though the jack-o'-lantern mushroom might try.

When you find one, get down on your hands and knees. Look uphill. Usually others are peeking out from under the eaves.

Galbiori: yellowish one, Romanian. *Rubito*: little blond, Spanish.

Lanterns on dark water.

Over the course of about a month, they continue to evolve, growing larger, adding layers of *basidia* ("little pedestals"), the spore-bearing organs of their underbellies. Often they come as twins. Just pick one, it's suggested, so the second may propagate.

Sporulate.

So the other may remember its lover.

(But, the temptation.)

~⌒~

Reach into the earth and pinch the mushroom's base. Twist gently, so as not to damage the white hairs running everywhere through the scalp.

Another nickname: *girolle* in France, from *girer*. "Little twist."

Dwo-

Twilight. Twelfth night. The twig, which splits in two. A dozen golden biscuits. Balanced between pinochle and diploma. And never the twain shall meet.

Duet.

I think of Keats: "Heard melodies are sweet, but those unheard / Are sweeter; therefore, ye soft pipes, play on . . ."

Take up this chanterelle and run your fingers lightly across the flutes and ridges that climb from the stalk to the bottom of the cap.

Pleated, like the throat of baleen whales off the coast, those rorquals that gulp thirty tons of sea at a time and then squeeze, filtering planktonic life.

At the foot of giant trees, on the margins of redwood canyons, chanterelles surface all at once and breathe awhile.

The undersurface of a mushroom, which bears the spores, is known as the "hymenium." Most have gills, thin as knife blades, but chanterelles have only "blunt folds."

Hymenium, from the Greek diminutive for "membrane": *humēn*.

Mem-: meat, flesh.

⌒‿⌒

Then the jaunt back to the kitchen. A loose-weave basket is recommended for carrying mushrooms, because it helps scatter spores as you go, seeding the forest.

Clean them with a brush. Sweep away dirt, bits of leaf and grass. Rinse quickly, if you need to, so the mushrooms don't absorb too much water, diluting their potency.

Pare off any rot, those soft discolored pieces. On a tired specimen, one ready to melt back into the earth, the ribs of the hymenium—those blunt folds—will break easily, mushing under a fingernail.

Glistening when wet. Covered with fine, white hairs when dry, like the fuzz on an apricot: canescence. The chanterelle also rises from a dark pit.

Canescence, from the proto-Indo-European root *Kas-*: gray. *Kas-no* becoming the Latin *cānus*, "white, gray-haired"; becoming also the Germanic *hazōn*, becoming "hare."

Oreille de lièvre, hare's ear. The French have so many wonderful endearments.

Lay the tender slices altogether in a hot pan; let the rain cook off and condense on the ceiling overhead. Add butter. A splash of chardonnay. Salt, pepper.

Shallots, perhaps.

So many eggs, cracked open in the forest. *Jidanhuang*, in Chinese: egg yolk.

The Czech *kuratko*: chick. The Portuguese *canarinhos*: canary bird, chicken. The Italian *galletto*: young rooster.

⌒⌒

When a covey is found, you might hear a brief crowing in the woods: chanticleer, in boots.

Which brings us to the proto-Indo-European *Kan-*: to sing. Which became the Germanic *han(e)ni*, which was destined to lay "hen."

Which also begot the Latin *canare* or *cantus*: Charm. Sweet canorous cant. Canto, cantata. Accent and enchant. Incentive to recant.

"Chanties," the mushroom gatherers say, affectionately. Songs of labor.

So it occurred that, from two separate roots, or spores, the same word arose: In French, a *chanterelle* was also a decoy bird, the melodic female partridge used to draw in others of its species during the hunt.

Now obsolete. But the chanterelle remains the topmost string on an instrument, the ethereal note. The thumbstring on a lute.

I see it's *ull de perdiu* in Catalonian: partridge eye.

As for "shanty," it comes from the Canadian French *chantier*: "a lumberjack's cabin," "logging camp," "the headquarters at which the woodcutters assemble after a day's work."

"Since you have been here," Melville wrote to a friend, and perhaps an unrequited love, "I have been building some shanties of houses (connected with the old one) and likewise some shanties of chapters and essays. I have been plowing and sowing and raising and painting and printing and praying . . ."

These days, I walk carefully through the woods, tiptoeing across the soft ground. Hopping like a wren from log to log. Knowing that I compress, year by year, making it more difficult for mushrooms to spring up.

~‿~

A season without chanterelle is a season of terrible drought.

But in a really good year, drive to Kmart and buy an electric dehydrator for $29.99.

Dried, they are still divine, to my mind. You can also simply lay the slices flat on a cookie sheet. Slide them onto the middle rack, bake at a low temperature. The caps will shrivel and brown to a handful of spiced petals.

Fragrant potpourri: "rotten pot," a stew of miscellaneous meat.

Always keep a jar in the pantry. Twist off the lid and inhale the desiccated year.

An hour in a bowl of warm water is all that's needed. Then stir into risotto. Add to cream, pour over pasta. The flavor is condensed, but the bites can sometimes be chewy.

Season slowly. Eat light.

The Kurgan nomads take their name from the tumuli or burial mounds, the "kurgans," that they left in their wake. It's a Russian word from a Turkic origin that means "castle."

Crenellation on amber ramparts. Projectiles whistling down. Tumulus, from *Teu-*: to swell. Tuber and truffle, tomb and thumb.

When chanterelles first emerge, they mound the leaf litter, pushing up the earth and sometimes through. Rake your hands across these hillocks to find the color.

Yet another derivative of chanterelle's root, *Kemb-*: the Germanic "hump."

⌒‿⌒

In their kurgans, the ancient pastoralists buried cinerary urns; it's believed that, seasonally, they disinterred their recent dead to cremate them and rebury their ancestors in these ceremonial earthworks that, even today, interrupt the endless plains.

Just as a fungus recycles and lifts skyward. Saprophyte: the Greek *sapros*, "putrid" and *phuton*, "a plant."

From *phuein*, "come into being."

"He that lay in a golden Urne eminently above the Earth, was not likely to finde the quiet of these bones," Sir Thomas Browne observed. "Where profit hath prompted, no age hath wanted such miners."

In Europe, you may find the ashen chanterelle, *Cantharellus cinereus*, with a hymenium that is deeply folded, gray, thick with veins.

Not a chanticleer then, but a phoenix.

In North America, a black chanterelle also rises like a slender finger of soil: *Craterellus cornucopioides*. It proves difficult to spot, blending in with the gloom. Horn of plenty, it's called, along the Pacific Coast. *Trompette-de-la-mort* in France.

Shadow flower, I might like to name it.

The proto-Indo-European *Ker-*: horn, head. Giving rise to cornea, cornet. Hornet. Corn on the cob, on the foot. The antler-like carrot and its carotene. Cranium, carat. Cervid and hart.

The Germans also imagine it a *rehfüsshen*, deer's foot. And it's true: chanterelle does often grow just beside, or even on, their narrow, wandering trails.

~⌒~

Hidalgo, Mexico: *corneta*.

What this horn plays is winter, is water percolating through loam, is the inevitability of driest summer and empty hands.

Is our need to carry on and play.

Keats again: "Pipe to the spirit ditties of no tone: / Fair youth, beneath the trees, though canst not leave / Thy song, nor ever those trees be bare . . ."

Chanterelles pour into us: beta-carotene and other carotenoids, their orange, from which vitamin A is made. They're also a source of vitamin D that is second only to cod liver oil.

Chinese herbalists prescribe chanterelle to treat night blindness.

Pull off a leaf, once wet and now plastered tight to the cap, and a pale silhouette remains like an imprint on skin, just before the blood returns.

Mãozinhas: baby hands, Portuguese.

It's thought that the carotenoids of a golden chanterelle help the mushroom grope toward light. Toward open space, new edges: those treefall gaps where saplings will themselves.

Only recently, my native chanterelle was recognized as its own species, and so given a new name: *Cantharellus californicus*, "the oak chanterelle." It's the largest in the world, as it turns out, and I'd say the most delicious.

Probably it tastes like the San Andreas Fault.

~~~~~

"When we think of the unending growth and decay of life and civilizations," wrote Carl Jung, "we cannot escape the impression of absolute nullity. Yet I have never lost the sense of something that lives and endures beneath the eternal flux. What we see is blossom, which passes. The rhizome remains."

Thus it begins, in a wet moment: The spore's wall becomes permeable. The cell absorbs. A "germ tube" forms, enlarging with protoplasm, sending the first hypha into the matrix in search of an association. Some rootlet to coil around.

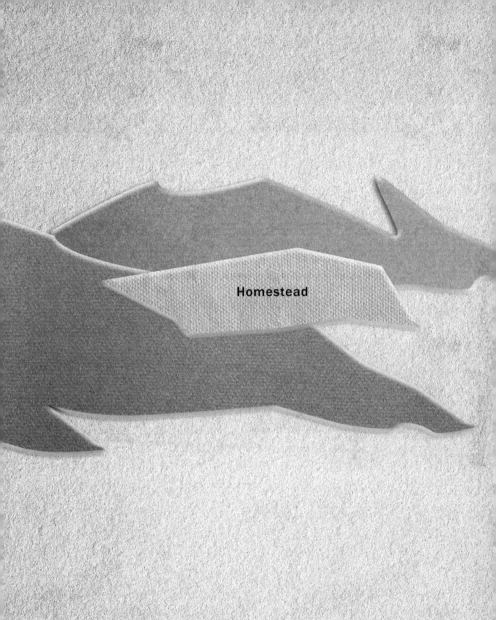

Homestead

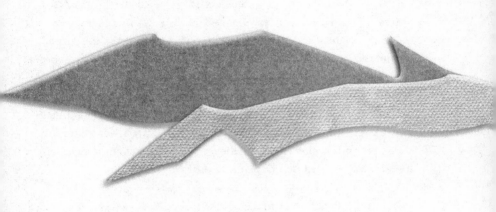

When we peeled back the tarps in the garden, snakes slithered in every direction: a large gopher snake, garters, a fast racer. The earth was clayey, hard-caked, and Sarah and I would need to turn it over if our starters and seeds from Grants Pass were to have a chance. We revved up the aged rototiller, and I churned the largest bed, more or less, before it quit on us and stood there for several days, under one of those same tarps, a heavy monument shrouded in black. What would

Bradley do, we always said. What we did was roll it into the barn, for good, another casualty of time and probably misuse. Fat chance I would be able to fix it.

The other beds we tilled with a shovel, and I even dug a new one, cutting the sod and tossing it to the side. They looked like the unmarked graves of giants. Brussels sprouts and basil, rows of carrots, beets, onions. Tomatoes and broccoli. In the corner nearest the tall fir and walnut tree, we planted lettuce, where it would receive a few extra hours of natural shade, and I made a diaphanous canopy from dowels and spare bug netting to help keep them cool. We made little craters with mounds at their center, as if, in red clay, sculpting the mountain that gave birth to the Rogue, and planted our squash starters, our melon and cucumber and zucchini. We filled them with cold water and watched as it sank away, headed for our plates or the river.

The meadow lay like a leaf fallen in the forest. It was about five acres, sweeping down a southeast-facing slope on a diagonal, absorbing the harsh summer light of the Rogue River Canyon, a couple of hours' drive west of Grants Pass and the nearest grocery store. It was known as the Dutch Henry Homestead, and before that, as one of the Little Meadows. The cabins were perched on its upslope edge, the Boydens' and ours, the residents'.

I had been selected for a six-month writing residency off the grid in the backcountry of southern Oregon. Sarah and I had visited in the fall to see what we were getting into and meet Bradley and Frank Boyden, the brothers who owned this remote and ideal property. We had stayed at the upper cabin then, the Boydens' original with cedar shake siding, and absorbed the impressive seesaw view across the conifer to Rattlesnake Ridge, the unseen Rogue below, and Big Windy Mountain in the distance. The canyon was starkly V-shaped, velvet with forest, three thousand feet from the ridgetop to the river, which runs over two hundred miles from the shield of Crater Lake to the town of Gold Beach on the Pacific.

Downhill from the upper cabin's deck was Dutch Henry's original apple orchard: small trees more than a hundred years old, askew and gnarled, ravaged to gnomes by wind and the bears. Knee-high ferns crept out from the woods just there, in the shadow of the forest's edge, green when we arrived, then frittered to brown and rust red as the year burned. Young firs had grown unnoticed among the fronds, but now peeked above this spore-filled canopy. The meadow was an old fire scar, and this is how a meadow closes in: everyone in turn taking cover in each other's shade, then outgrowing it, ad infinitum.

Other people had lived on the homestead before us. Other people had broken and tended this ground. The Takelma and Shasta Costa tribes made their home along the Rogue River until 1856, when they were routed and marched to coastal reservations. Dutch Henry, a hard-scrabble miner, had been the first to hole up permanently on this meadow in the 1880s, and a man by the name of Bill Graiff had continued on after him. The Boydens had bought the homestead from Graiff's heirs in 1968 and, for a long time, hired summer caretakers, some of them liabilities, until in 1992 they began the residency program. I was the eighteenth recipient of this backcountry stay.

The homestead was an inholding in the federally designated Wild and Scenic corridor of the Rogue. To find it, we drove west from Grants Pass to Galice, which was once a mining outpost and is now a resort, gas pump, and raft launch. We crossed the Rogue on the concrete bridge at Grave Creek, where Martha Leland Crowley, a daughter of early settlers, was buried under a lone oak along the stream in 1846. Here the Wild and Scenic portion of the river began, as the road's steep grade essentially declared. You began to wind up the canyon's precarious north slope, under blasted rock and spiraled, leaning madrone. The drop was sheer and ended in the single thread, frayed with white, that was the Rogue held in its greenstone.

The pavement relinquished to gravel. We turned north, away from the Rogue to a pass at thirty-eight hundred feet; then down another ridge, back to the river, on a road Dutch Henry had pioneered as a mule trail to Glendale, where he took his orchard fruit for sale. The Rogue journeys through the Siskiyou Mountains, in a region known as the Klamath Knot that straddles the California-Oregon border. This unforgiving territory is one of the most ancient and complex places in Oregon, or anywhere: It is, in fact, a collection of island arcs and continental fragments—ocean-drifting mountains, like Japan—that collided with North America between four hundred and two hundred million years ago. Driving into the homestead, I always felt as if I were tracing one strand of the knot to its fossil core.

Bradley Boyden had "installed" us over the course of a few days in early June. A biology teacher in Portland, he is the youngest of the Boyden brothers, gregarious and jovial, bald and mustached. He showed us how to unlock the BLM gate, how to solder a copper pipe, how to screw up slightly less. He walked us through the wood's dry madrone leaves to follow the spring-fed water and irrigation system he had built. He demonstrated that it was perfectly acceptable, preferable even, to use a fishing exclamation for life in general: "Good action!" He told stories to put the fear of the Rogue in us, and reminded us how to play cribbage late at night with whiskey, in the glow of kerosene.

Bradley showed us the trails, including the route to Horseshoe Bend, a famous turn in the Rogue, a near circle. On the hike, I tried to make it look as though I knew how to carry a chainsaw over my shoulder; a few trees were down, nothing huge, and Bradley showed us how to saw through safely and chaperoned as we took our requisite whirl. Horseshoe Bend was a beaut: The river wraps around a durable volcanic intrusion, a conical hill of madrone and oak. Someday the Rogue will punch through and leave it an island, but for now the river swings reluctantly through a stone channel painted with faded waterlines, bathtub rings in the wilderness.

Bradley showed us the site of the tiny cabin, on an old mining claim beside Horseshoe Bend, that his family had leased summers when he was a boy. He and his brothers would boat twenty-five miles downriver from Galice with their mother, Margery, and on weekends their father, Allen, a surgeon in Portland, would fly in on a bush plane and land at Black Bar. The Boydens were soon woven into the canyon's rough-hewn and self-reliant community. Once, for example, Bradley's father was called upon when a fisherman took a double hook through his eye on a backcast. With another doctor, he stayed up all night to practice extracting the curved steel from an apple by lamplight. I picture him picking the redolent fruit, an eye, and tossing it lightly in his hand with that leaden calm in his stomach. In the morning, he performed the surgery. The angler kept his eye.

These were the stories that echoed, though now the cabin clearing held nothing but warped and splintered planks, tins, a rusted and off-kilter bed frame. The Boydens had to give up this summer home when the canyon was labeled "Wild and Scenic" and much of the evidence of its former use was erased. The Forest Service burned many of the old miners' cabins. It was then that the homestead came into their picture, and so into ours.

The Boydens befriended a trapper and miner, Red Keller, who lived in the canyon, and they enlisted him to watch over the Horseshoe Bend cabin when they were away, and to show the kids how one might properly explore and survive off the land. How to fish, and track, and roll a cigarette with the translucent, auburn curls of madrone bark, which peel from the tree like shavings under a lathe. The brothers used to shoot the invasive bullfrogs in the algal ponds behind the Bend for marksmanship. They would simply explode, said Bradley. As the youngest, it was his job to swim out and bring their legs home for supper. It was also here that Bradley shot and dressed his first and only deer, and hung it up to cure in the cabin above their cots, where the bears couldn't get it. But the flies could.

On a bookshelf in our cabin was a volume of local and oral history, *Illahe*, the name of a town further down the Rogue and a word that, in the Chinook language, means "land," "home," "the place where one resides." From its pages, the Rogue's turn-of-the-century inhabitants spoke to us. We learned about Dutch Henry, and we found Red Keller there, too. In a photograph, he peered out at us as if through a cabin window: wisps of white hair on either side of his bald pate, a wide nose, and a forehead with wrinkles like the crevices in which he hunted gold. In his seventies, he is shirtless and standing before a wall of fir poles, some cabin of his.

Red hiked into the Rogue in 1934 when he was twenty-five, one year older than us when we were given the keys to the homestead's gates. He never left, scraping out a living from the river. There were a few homesteads like ours in the hills, but Red stayed low in the canyon, moving along the river according to his whim and luck in mining. He wasn't a homesteader, in this sense, but he knew this stretch. It was his home, his stead. I imagine his smoker's voice as having the quality of the Rogue's immense shade.

"First thing I look for in a cabin site is whether I can get water close," said Red in *Illahe*. "Then pick the site high enough. I have to pick it where I know I can get wood. . . . What you need is a good big dead snag you can fall. I like my site where I can get the sun. That's what I like about Horseshoe Bend. You don't get the sun real early, but you get all the late sun. Winter, if there was any sun, you got it." Early miners built cabins swiftly and moved between them like water in a flood. Often they resided in them for just one season. That described us.

We kept the mowers and shovels under the porch. Like the upper cabin, the lower was stilted: Digging a true foundation in this wilderness would be quite the chore. After the long road in, we steered the Jeep up a short, final driveway, tall with grass when we arrived, and parked in front of a green woodshed. The cabin was somewhat mongrel, added onto in stages, with a gabled, A-shaped roof. Bradley had spent a summer building the cabin's core in the eighties. You entered the annex kitchen through an anteroom clogged with garden equipment and a defunct hand-cranked laundry machine. We would take our clothes to town when we drove out every two weeks.

In the main room, a green-and-white topographic map, the Horseshoe Bend quadrangle, was tacked above our local library: three shelves. There was a cinnamon couch, an orange chest for a coffee table and footrest, and a La-Z-Boy. A sliding glass door opened with a slurp to the porch, and beside it was the worn kitchen table where I sometimes wrote in a retired office chair. The chair was hidden under a patterned slip cloth that gave the seat its name: the Route 66 Distinguished Chair in Creative Writing. Every resident had leaned back in it.

For energy, we had a solar panel that fed two car batteries nestled behind the couch, which were wired to several LEDs and a power strip. When the column of indicator lights fell from green, to yellow, to red, reminding us of the traffic lights we had left far behind, we would desist to avoid harming the battery. If it was sunny, we had mountains of energy. If it was overcast, we rationed, fell deeper into the valley. Sometimes we had none, but then there were propane and kerosene lamps to read by. Our solar panel also powered a radiophone. We were far too gone for cables. The entire Rogue Canyon shared one frequency and, if you picked up the receiver, you could listen in on the distant end of the conversation, which we enjoyed on Father's Day: *You're the greatest, Dad. Over.*

Our bedroom was in the rear, with a low skylight that caused us to dream wildly in the morning. The back eave was flush to the hillside, and I often imagined a mountain lion looking in on us, or just its silhouette in the stars. That first month, the moon. Then I dragged a tarp from the garden and covered us like the weeds that would need to be suppressed before next season. We slept much better. Maybe too well. There was another window along the bank, a diorama lush with forbs and tiny ferns. One morning, I remember waking to find a ripe strawberry dangling there, the size of a jellybean.

But to dwell on the cabin is to describe the lesser part of our experience. The cabin was cozy if utilitarian, but it opened to the Rogue. Those sliding glass doors were an irresistible invitation to the outside, as all sliding glass doors are. Beyond the garden, the meadow swelled upslope, foreshortened, silky, and cut with stands of bramble, before it fell into the trees that fell into the creek that was our home drainage. If the wind was subdued, you could hear the Rogue in its own long-traveled bed, way down. Evenings, the receding light on Rattlesnake Ridge looked like an orange eyelid of night gradually opening.

Rattlesnake Ridge had no name, in reality. Only a number on certain maps. But one of the first residents called it Rattlesnake after he rode his mountain bike fast down the jeep trail along its spine and noticed that a lot of sticks seemed to be kicking up into his rubber tires. These were rattlers, he later realized, striking at his spokes as he whirred by. But there was no recent memory of rattlesnakes in the meadow, though a dusty jar of rattles, those glorified scales, rested on the kitchen sill of the Boyden's upper cabin. We saw only those ophidians that emerged from the tarps, and once a delicate ring-necked snake, slate green-gray with a fiery collar and belly. It corkscrewed its tail as we lifted it, bluffing toxicity.

You couldn't see the upper cabin from the lower, so it felt as if this view was wholly ours. We couldn't refuse it. I spent many hours on the porch staring into the ample space, keeping time with the trees, which moved at the meadow's edge as if caressing each other. The tan oaks were especially mobile, *anemones*: "daughters of the wind." But also the fir and the madrones. All moved in a slow swirl so that areas of a single tree circulated variously—some sections pushed, others rebounding—and, looking at them, you could rarely discern the nature, the direction, of the breeze.

The porch was our fulcrum. Sarah set up a drawing table on one side; I read and wrote in a rocker on the other. There were also two patio chairs, a glass coffee table, a hammock, and a listless smoker, which was simply two rusty buckets welded together with vents in their sides. An unsteady plywood table was propped against the cabin wall, and on it, specimens: a cup of brass .22 shells from a recent poet who, for solitary entertainment, liked to take potshots at a snag over the garden; a ponderosa pinecone, enormous and tan; an antler the color of dry grass; a baby blue kerosene lamp with a pollen-dusted globe; and a paperback dictionary, abandoned, on the verge of collapse.

When you hang a hummingbird feeder in the wilderness, it's like building a McDonald's on a faraway mountain, only the customers are so zealous they try to bar the door and defend the place from all others. Ours was classic: plastic ruby-red with yellow florets. Without a doubt, it was the most garish object for twenty miles. The birds arrived within hours and began to parry each other's jousts. They didn't intuit that this well of sugar water would be bottomless for the season, though I suppose they, or even we, couldn't be sure we wouldn't walk into the woods and never return.

These were rufous hummingbirds, and one iridescent male in particular dominated the porch and our attention. We called him Ru, but the name stood for them all in the way that, for us, most individual animals, wild at least, more or less represent the species. Sometimes I would sit in the rocking chair, scarcely seven or eight feet from the feeder, and make them giant through the spotting scope I had brought. Every feather, I could see, almost every barbule. Ru was all ruddy—rufous—with a green back and crown, and a hammered-copper gorget that flared to a gleaming razor's edge. He was a gorgeous tyrant. He would dive in, with a metallic slur, and drive away the less showy males; or he would display for a female, cornering her and forcing her to sit on the porch's wire railing while he fanatically waved, thrusted, his loud tail.

A clothesline ran from one side of the porch to a pole above the old smokehouse turned chicken coop, turned blackberry rest. When we went to Grants Pass, we would haul our clothes wet from the laundromat across from Safeway—we shopped while they agitated—and once we returned to the canyon, we'd string them out using a pulley. They looked like the tattered prayer flags some former resident had hung in the porch's rafters. Ru and company utilized this line also, perching there in the sun—sometimes two or three at a time, if they were feeling amicable—above this low corner of meadow. They loved clothes. When Sarah or I wore a bright T-shirt, they'd startle us with their investigations.

We would rise, not too early, shovel coffee into a plastic cone, and listen to the river percolate in the windless distance. I would head to the porch, my station. Like a lookout, I felt compelled to survey, to see what had changed in the meadow overnight. Maybe today there would be a bear, or a tree might have fallen, or the weather would signal. I spent countless hours in the rocker, sometimes with my laptop, until I had to set it aside to train the spotting scope on a western tanager or lazuli bunting, or a fawn in the hoof steps of its original home. In the heat of the day, I might retreat to the creaky Route 66 chair and fewer distractions.

Sarah would venture forth most days and endeavor to bring order to the visual disorder that is the forest as you continue to stare: the landscape alternately shifting from chaos to symmetry, an oscillation without beginning or end; the trees comfortably nestled from afar, a jumble closer in; radially balanced up their trunks, but each branch perfectly irregular. For her, the canvas was a backcountry of its own, and she had to come to her plein air survival skills by trial and error, and color. And always by trees, her passion.

The same for me, and I was not only in search of technique and style, and rhythm. I had come with a project, one set in Rhode Island, but staring across the meadow to Rattlesnake Ridge, the vastness of the continent was palpable. The clouds drifted away slowly, like an Oregon Trail in reverse, billowy covered wagons. At the same time, I was hesitant to write about the homestead. More experienced writers than me had called it home. Several books had been written about this slant of ground, this meadow scar. What territory was left to cover, and was it mine?

Homesteading, of course, has a storied history in Oregon. In 1850, Congress passed the Oregon Donation Land Law, which lifted more dust on the braided trail westward. This was when Oregon was all of the Northwest, *Ouragun*, apparently a Native name for the region's one great river, now known as the Columbia. Under the act, 320 acres were "granted to every white settler or occupant of the public lands, American half-breed Indians included, above the age of eighteen years, being a citizen of the United States, or having made a declaration according to law of his intention to become a citizen." Not just "half-breeds" and immigrants, but also the wives of settlers, one of the first times in U.S. history that women were allowed property.

It was a progressive law, in this light. Together, a couple could claim 640 acres, a full square mile. You had to live and improve upon the land for four years to gain legal title. After 1850, portions were halved, and after 1855, each acre cost a dollar and a quarter. So people were encouraged into the territories. They were given their shot at self-reliance while extending the reach and clout of the nation. To a small degree, this was also our contract on the Rogue. For two seasons, we were given property and shelter, and inspiration, and in return we would help defend and reclaim the meadow from the encroaching woods. We would be caretakers.

Three times a week, Sarah and I would break in the afternoon to spend at least an hour on some chore, our only requirement. The list, in the resident's manual we inherited from Bradley, was considerable: Sweep needles from all roofs. Pull thistle. Rake leaves away from cabins, and out from under them. Mow the road and its shoulders. Mow a perimeter around the cabins for a fire buffer. Prune the two rows of grapevines. Weed the garden's strawberry patch, that unlikely island of delectableness. Spray poison oak—eradicate it. Weed the pond's edges. Shore up and improve the drainage ditches on the road. Keep the trails clear. Check the springhouse for leaks and dead mice . . .

Sometimes we would split up, but if the work was arduous or involved covering ground, we worked together. Or nearby. I remember hearing Sarah scrape at the moss on the upper cabin's tarpaper roof as I uprooted those furtive saplings in the cloud forest of ferns below Dutch Henry's apples, and enjoying the rasp of her effort, the two-step of my shovel. It was true that the chores brought us closer to the homestead, made it feel like a home rather than a visitation. We had invested not only our time, but also modest labor in the land, and in doing the work, we learned more of its corners. Earned them. Western skinks swam in electric blue though the oak leaves, as did alligator lizards with a more menacing visage and bite. For a week, grasshoppers fled in waves before our steps like the crackling of fire. The birds descended to feast on their horned bodies.

Below our cabin, a feeble pole-and-shake barn with cedar shingles stood that once had kept Bill Graiff's mules. Later in our tenure, we found a ladder and raked the heavy mat of needle from its bowed, tenuous eaves. All we could reach, anyway. There was no climbing onto those wings. We had to leave one patch at center, which we hoped in time would slide down instead of becoming a planter for young fir. Under this picturesque roof was nothing much: stacks of scrap lumber and tarped equipment, the rusted albatross of the rototiller; but everything is potentially useful when you're that far gone.

In June, however, the barn became the meadow's center of life, the focus of our attention: Three gray fox kits emerged. Inside the barn, under one of those stacks, was a den, a warm, uric hold. They had short snouts and charcoal masks that grew bolder over time and gave them a

scoundrelly appearance. Around the barn, they ran, wagging and yip-
ping softly. Up woodpiles and off. We watched them wrestle in, and
with, the tufted grass. We watched all this through the scope, our handy
portal to the greater meadow. The porch couldn't have been a better
observation deck: just far enough from the barn that they couldn't see
us, could hardly smell us.

There was no male, just a mother. She was silvered as pine bark and
sometimes, somehow sensing us, she would stand extraordinarily still,
statuesque, staring in our general direction or just slant. Whole morn-
ings the kits were hidden and silent, and then she would return, giving
a soft bark on approach. The eager kits would emerge, and we would
emerge to watch, and they would surround her, dog-piling to nurse as
she stood vigilant. One day the mother returned with her eye swollen
shut; she had injured it somehow, a branch maybe, and we wondered
what this meant for her hunting and the kits. But it healed. The kits
played under those eaves as if the barn had been built for them. They
kept to the rear mostly, until suddenly two would spill from behind,
scamper and tumble, and race back. Inside the barn, tendrils of fur and
scat covered the swept ground. They grew bigger. Then they were gone.

We knew the bears were coming. The garden was perhaps the most
fortified in Oregon: steel posts far thicker than my arm, strung with
barbwire. An electric wire traced the perimeter. It looked like a prison
for tomatoes. The solar-powered charge box for the wire, set on a post
inside the garden like a birdhouse, produced a quiet tick as we weeded
the strawberries. From the wire, you could hang a matchbook-sized
tray with a sinister dab of peanut butter, but Sarah and I are softies.
In fact, I thought about putting my hand to the wire also, to feel what
might course through that great wet nose, tightening the muscles and
the mind, but I never worked up the nerve for that, either.

One of the chores Bradley left us was to add a layer of six-foot deer
fence along the base of the existing garden fence, so the bears couldn't
dig under. Their habit was to raid the garden and gorge on the resident's hopes and dreams, namely apples. You think of bears as expert
climbers, but they excavate just as well. For grubs, those claws will
tear open a log in seconds flat; we'd seen the shredded evidence in the

woods. We tied the new fence length into the existing, fastening it with wire, and bent it at a right angle along the ground. Our fingers grew sore from the twisting. On a vice in the shed, I then bent rebar into U-shaped stakes and, with a maul, we drove these into the meadow, tamping down the skirt that the grass would soon devour.

A third of the way to river, past the trail's steepest grades, was the "love grove": a knoll with large firs, named by the Boydens for familial history. Now the main attraction was a beer cache dug into the ground. The pit had been lined loosely with brick, and another resident had fashioned a plywood hatch with hinges. Yellow-legged centipedes crawled at bottom. If there was enough daylight and the mosquitoes weren't thirsty, Sarah and I might stop and share a cold one; semi-cold. Maybe a Rogue Dead Guy Ale or a Sierra Nevada. It made the rest of the climb harder, but made it easier, too. We added to the well's refrigeration before we left by pouring a sip from our water bottles.

I mention the cache because, once, when we hadn't stopped in a while, Sarah and I discovered the hatch had been flipped off to the side. The beers were jostled, knocked about. Claw marks ran across one label. We toasted to this unexpected visitor, drank that pawed ale with a flourish, and gave the empty bottle a place of honor on our kitchen sill, among many Rogue-sculpted knots of wood known, for their incisor shape, as river teeth. Each morning, those long scratches on the bottle glowed amber, like a phrase etched in the glass itself; the bear was invited in to that extent.

If there were no pressing chores, we headed for the river. The trail was its own animal: a seven-hundred-foot descent in three-quarters of a mile; the switchbacks shorter and steeper higher up, longer and easier where the Rogue came to the ear and began to flicker through the windows of madrone and oak draped with Spanish moss. But none of it was easy. The north side of the canyon, our side, caught the light and had a rich diversity of trees, while the southern slope was sunless, primeval green, a tapestry of conifer. Walking fast, I could make the downhill in ten minutes, the uphill in thirteen. A relaxed pace was twenty.

We would join the official Rogue River Trail discreetly, to keep the route to the meadow and the cabins a secret. It was not uncommon to find bandana-clad backpackers or, especially, sunbaked rafters. Sometimes we would enjoy their rubber hoots, their shouts and paddle wars, as they drifted in the heat. Sometimes, naively, we wished this wilderness was only ours. In any case, we'd wave. Near the homestead's trail was a popular pullout and campsite below a lone pine. When we appeared, backpackers always wondered—even in how they looked us up and down—why we weren't crusted in sweat and dust, and packing a heavier load. We always said that we'd made camp nearby and left our stuff, which was basically the truth.

The banks of the river were summer-parched, but its tributaries were tunnels of fern. These side creeks were the Rogue's lifeblood and our resting places. Past that lone pine, soon the Rogue River Trail crossed a creek, the homestead's runoff, and I knew there must have been Native people living just here, where salmon used to linger in the frigid influx and backpackers now tent. In small numbers, the Shasta Costa Band of the Tututni tribe had lived in the Rogue Canyon to Grave Creek, where the territory of the Takelma began, extending east into the broad Rogue Valley toward Crater Lake.

They made their villages of four or five families on flat ground where streams joined the Rogue and created favorable microclimates, warmer in winter, cooler in summer. They relied on acorns, especially black oak, and on venison and salmon. Each family lived in a rectangular pit-house with its floor dug out several feet. Upright corner posts, crossbeams, a gable roof. Siding was hewn pine or, for the less well-off, rough bark—not very different from the pole-and-shake cabins of miners or the homestead's rickety barn. Smoke from the fire vented through the rafters, and the entrance was a low round hole that served several functions: A guest must bow in respect as he enters; a bear is too large to be a guest; and an enemy is unable to pass with his weapons lifted.

Our regular cove was just above the mouth of our home creek, with a view up-canyon a few miles to Rattlesnake Ridge. The river was dark olive, perhaps fifty feet wide, a swirling glass. Across it, an osprey nest leaned out in a fir, far too high to see inside of. It was an abandoned cabin, this year, but we saw them fishing and wheeling, and once harassing a bald eagle that dwarfed them. Dippers bobbed on the margins with nictitating eyelids and ran underwater, carrying the river on their slate shoulders. We saw otters several times, their svelte bodies like rogue waves. Red-breasted mergansers trailed the edges with their silent, precocious young. And once I flushed a spotted sandpiper from its nest under an eave of rock and grass: four pale eggs, speckled and tapered.

We would read and daydream in camp chairs rooted in the sand. Some days we would pack dinner in Tupperware, maybe pesto pasta and cucumber salad. We swam right off the beach, and several times I stroked across the heavy, slow-boiling current to climb out and plunge into the white funnel of a wave train. Sometimes we would float holding our sandals and, before the first rapid, swim to shore and scramble back. The bank's stone was burnished and black, slippery and dangerous when wet. There were potholes where it looked as if someone long ago had pounded a pestle to grind acorns. Some giant, must have been. But these cavities were the work of other stones, some of them still resting in their mortars, which had swirled and bore in vortices powered by higher water. Sometimes I found moths floating in them. Sometimes my own reflection.

The first Europeans in the Rogue country came for fur, before the other variety of fir came to be more valuable. A Hudson's Bay Company expedition led by Peter Skene Ogden crossed these mountains, the Siskiyous, to the broad Rogue Valley in 1827. They had no desire to call it home, but instead were intent on beaver, those fine-haired pelts most luxurious in winter, that "soft gold." He was among the French who gave this place its name: La Rivière aux Coquins, the River of Rogues.

There may have been some incidence of petty theft at the root of that moniker. But at least in English, a "rogue" was first an idle vagrant, and that's how the French saw the Shasta Costa and Takelma, who in summer left their modest plank villages along the river for the thawed mountains. There they gathered and hunted, sometimes stalking the meadows in an antlered disguise, and lived in shelters of brush or boughs. This is what home looked like in Oregon until the middle of the nineteenth century, but the French did not recognize it.

Fishing the Rogue below our home creek one afternoon, I spotted a plastic bottle wedged between boulders. But when I lifted this trash, it had two incisors stained golden with tannin: a beaver skull. We had not seen a beaver or its pond, though I knew they existed along the Rogue. "You see beaver now and then," Red Keller said. "They don't seem to stay all winter. They're in there in the pond at Horseshoe Bend. They chew willow."

We knew beaver had been nearly eliminated in Oregon, as in many places. Even those early trappers seemed to know it was a matter of time. In 1827, Peter Skene Ogden himself wrote of trapping in the Rogue country: "We have this day, eleven Beaver. It is almost a sin to see the number of Small Beaver we destroy and to no purpose. Some of the Females taken have no less than five young and on an average three each. In a month hence their young would be sent in to the world. This is the affect of Traps. It spares neither Male or Female. Almost equal to death, all are distroyed." This is not to say he felt for beaver, though maybe he did: Many trappers develop an unrivaled respect for their quarry. But just as likely he regretted the loss of those coats, or "plews."

I carried this beaver skull up the trail with my finger curled through a socket and placed it on the porch table. With shadow eyes, it stared at the meadow over my shoulder as I rocked. All summer, it sat beside the ruffled dictionary. I imagined its teeth lusting after the timber.

When we headed to Horseshoe Bend, we would take the Corral Trail. Downhill to the creek, to ferns and pools, then uphill, following the contour of the hillside as it dried to another, larger meadow: the Corral. The oldest trees held by this route and, inevitably, we would reach out and brush them with our fingertips. Passing one of these giants, you slow purposely or unconsciously. There were Doug fir wider than my six-foot arm span, some fire- or lightning-touched; and one barrel of a ponderosa, hard by the trail, that seemed marooned in the Rogue Canyon since the tree is mainly found farther east, the puzzle of its bark forever being disassembled and left in a pile.

Before the Corral, a pallid madrone leaned over the trail and, at eye level, there were the claw marks of a bear again, scars in the chilly tree. Bradley had showed us, letting us in on the scattered secrets of the place. We would pause here also, run our fingers through these lacquered grooves, these healed lacerations, and imagine the bear in our shoes, raised on its haunches and marking its territory. We would imagine it imagining us. Contemplating our scent. There the trail filled with leathery madrone leaves that unavoidably stirred and crunched underfoot, and I would cringe, thinking I'd just spooked a bear or mountain lion up ahead. The first lobe of the meadow swept downhill on the right, and I always had a premonition that something might be waiting there. It was one of those margins that just seems to cry out for good action.

At the center of the Corral Meadow was a spring-fed grove that really might have attracted a lion. Whorls of matted grass in the shade were the beds of deer. In a snag, tree swallows nested: their plumage evergreen above, right through the eye, and cloud-white below; the inverse of the world, they are camouflaged in flight no matter the per-spective. Near the grove, a round metal trough was nestled in reeds and sometimes partially filled with water as if the pack animals might soon arrive, Dutch Henry's or the Forest Service's: The government had grazed this meadow for years. Or it was as if the volunteer cavalry had just left in pursuit of the Takelma during the Rogue Indian Wars. Someone had slanted a board with rungs into the trough, a ladder for the mice and voles. So they wouldn't poison the water.

Walking through the Corral, we avoided the obvious poison oak but not the burrs. Several corral posts still stood, bleached and aslant. There was a honeysuckle tangle we watched come into leaf and even-tually simmer with hundreds of berries that looked like salmon eggs, only more blood-filled. Then we wandered down the slope of oaks that hid the Corral from the Rogue River Trail, where another landmark madrone grew, a behemoth Bradley called the Octopus Tree. Like most of us, the Boydens have many mythologies to help them find their way. Long ago, this octopus had swallowed, grown around, an iron stave that someone had forgotten or placed in a crutch.

It was the Donation Land Law that made the Rogue Indian Wars of 1855–1856 inevitable. The Rogue Wars, they should be called, since by no means were only Indians involved. Just before the act was passed,

Congress also set in motion the end of Indian title in the Northwest, hurrying the negotiation of unimaginably lopsided treaties, as usual. In Oregon, as everywhere, the land was already, and eloquently, spoken for, but settlers poured into the Willamette and Umpqua Valleys, and into the fertile Rogue Valley upstream and east of our canyon, where the discovery of gold in 1851 further stoked pioneers.

They claimed the choicest riverine land and drove the Takelma from their villages. Farmers cleared trees and erected split-rail fences to declare private property on the oak savannah the Takelma had foraged across and periodically burned to rekindle growth. The settlers culled deer and elk herds, and their hogs snuffled under oaks and scarfed up the acorns that the Rogue people had pounded, leached, and stored as flour. Miners ruined salmon and steelhead spawning gravels as they muddied the river with tailings. The only time we could properly imagine the color of that water was when, one day, Sarah and I arrived at the cove to find the Rogue completely "blown out" with silt, all brown. A dam had been removed upstream.

After skirmishes, the Takelma were cornered into a treaty that ceded the Rogue Valley for a postage-stamp reservation on Little Butte Creek, near the iconic Table Rocks: two tall mesas that are the only remnants of an ancient Rogue River's lava-filled meanders. But the winter of 1854 was severe, ravenous, diseased. When, the next year, one group of Takelma returned to the site of its former village, believing they couldn't withstand more banishment in the cold hills, settlers came down on them, while the men were away. They killed fifteen Takelma women and children.

The Takelma did what seems natural: They fled and took their revenge, heading west for the more inaccessible Rogue Canyon, ours, hoping to find solidarity with other bands. They killed several settlers they encountered before attacking the mining outpost at Galice with flaming arrows. Then into the canyon, likely on the same route later improved by the Forest Service to create the Rogue River Trail that we walked daily. They trailed past Whiskey Creek, before it was Whiskey Creek, and arrived at Black Bar, before a Mr. William Black gave it his name. There, just a few miles upstream of the homestead's location, the volunteer militia caught up with the Takelma and planned a stealthy attack. But their axes gave them away as they fell trees to rope up as rafts and drift across, and the Takelma escaped downstream for the winter.

Below our cabin was a hidden back trail to Kelsey Creek that, in places, seemed to have been carved from the hillside by pick or dynamite. But it had the feel of an old Indian trail, and maybe it was. We were in the footsteps of not only Dutch Henry. All these trails ebbed and flowed, it was clear. They were deer trails to begin with, and when humans forgot them for a time, the deer would keep their memory until they could be rediscovered, "improved" once more. It was our stead to keep them for a season. Several days, I wandered down the trail with brush cutters, but it was the act of walking them, of treading, that was most important.

Kelsey Creek was named for Colonel John Kelsey, who, in the spring of 1856, led the militia's cavalry in renewed pursuit of the Takelma. Two hundred volunteers rode into the canyon at Grave Creek to the vicinity of our Little Meadows. Probably they rested their horses at the Corral while scouting farther. A few miles downstream, the fugitive Takelma, winter-weary again, were camped along the Rogue. Kelsey led his men across the creek that would bear his name and, as the Takelma swam across the Rogue, launched volleys from higher ground, killing about thirty braves on what is now Battle Bar. It was the Takelma's first loss since Table Rocks and, in this second, short year of the Rogue Wars, it would spell the end of their resistance. One more skirmish at Big Bend, then a trail of rain to the Siletz Reservation north on the coast.

We swam naked in the cold of Kelsey Creek the first time we took that old, hidden trail from our meadow, not knowing this history, nor that the main, well-trafficked Rogue River Trail was in plain sight. The stream was an avenue of alder littered with sun. Ferns cradled the boulders. Bradley had told us that sometimes you could see salmon below Kelsey's sculpted mouth if you crept up on your belly. In all the Rogue's streams, there were rainbow trout, striders, others we couldn't imagine. Probably there were Pacific giant salamanders, though we never found them. They grow to more than a foot long and, as juveniles, have feathery gills to trap the air as it tumbles. For the rest of their life, they go terrestrial, a mottled, breathing log under a log. They're known to bark like a canine. They breed in underground springs.

My brother and his girlfriend visited in August, and we hiked to Kelsey Creek to camp, sleeping on a tarp in the open air. Just in case, we set our food at a distance. The night was cold, dewy, and I remember reeling in and out of half sleep's gray, sensing or imagining that something was near, that the gray was condensing. On the hike, we had seen bear shit the violet of lupines.

Back at the homestead, I slung my pack down and went into the garden to start the sprinkler across the wilting beds. The *chit, chit, chit* and shimmering arc always made us feel we had carved out a pastoral niche from the Rogue, when really it had fallen to us like this artificial rain. After the sweaty hike, I paused in the sifting water, let it coat my dusty skin. But when I climbed the cabin's steps and joined the others on the porch, something was amiss. Everyone was grim.

They had found a hummingbird hanging limp from the feeder, its bill lodged in the small plastic corolla. They had left it hanging there. It was a female Ru, with only a speckling of iridescence on her throat. I took her down and held her nickel-weight in my palm. Maybe another hummer had winged in, and she had darted too abruptly, instead of withdrawing her bill. The more awful possibility was that she had struggled in the yellow flower, a blur, until she wrenched or exhausted herself.

Why had this occurred while we were away, we wondered. Would it have happened if we'd been at the cabin? Would we have heard? Sarah and I felt guilty that our best intentions had trapped this bird, light and insignificant as it was. We unhooked the feeder and returned it to the cupboard with a note: *Warning: In 2009, a hummer's bill got stuck in the feeder, and it broke its neck. Use at your own karmic risk.* I probably should have buried the hummingbird or flung it into the woods, but instead I placed it—the shell of it, lighter than ever—on the table behind the rocker, thinking that others might study it, that something could be salvaged.

Dutch Henry was one of those men who swept into the Rogue country after the Takelma's removal. He wasn't Dutch, in fact, but a bow-legged German named Henry Rosenbrook who wandered into the canyon in the 1860s to scratch out gold, which is rarely a living. Then he turned Rogue, in the modern sense of the word. In 1875, he was mining with a partner near Kelsey Creek, when a series of arguments erupted. They ended when Dutch Henry raised his rifle butt and bashed his partner in the head, three times, killing him. There were eyewitnesses; one testified. Incredibly, Henry got off.

Then, in the early winter of 1881, a hairless body washed out of the Rogue's mouth: a tall man with a bloodless gash on his throat—a severe knife wound—as well as two missing fingers on his right hand, the pinkie and the ring. The *Port Orford Post* reported that this "drowned or murdered" man was a Mr. William Black, Dutch Henry's mule-packing partner. It soon came to light: While Dutch Henry was off with the mules, Black had absconded with Henry's "Indian woman." But not for long. Dutch Henry was tied and taken to Gold Beach to stand trial, where Black's lacerated head was presented as evidence. But again wily Dutch Henry walked free up the Rogue, successfully claiming self-defense. Black had rushed him with an ax, he said. Then he had the gumption to file for Black's mining claim, just above Horseshoe Bend: Black Bar.

Later in life, Dutch Henry moved upslope to the homestead's meadow with a modest herd of longhorns that, by legend, were more cantankerous than the bears. Bush cattle. They were the mowers once, circulating among the apples and staring, like me, from the shade at the meadow's edge. Dutch Henry must have settled down and turned generous, because the community seems to have remembered him fondly. In his dotage, he was cared for by an Austrian immigrant, Bill Graiff, who had left his wife and family for the Rogue.

Graiff remained at the homestead when Henry died in 1920, and he earned official title. After one of the great floods—before the river was dammed—Graiff collected doors, windows, and other essentials wrecked on the banks and built a proper house, wallpaper and all, in the middle of the meadow, as if to see every edge. A house, you might say, is the center of an eddy. In fact, Graiff's domicile was rather fancy. Red Keller described the typical residence in the canyon: "Most people down in there just built their own cabins. One person could build the pole-and-shake cabin. You stand your poles up and then you put your poles crossways to put your shakes on, and your roof too. Nothing real heavy, but it'll stand up for a long time. Most cabins had dirt floors because no air will come in when it's dirt. Sometimes you cooked outside. One place they just took tin cans and sleeved them together and that was the chimney."

Graiff went so far as to feed his home electricity: two bulbs, from a miniature turbine in the stream that flowed more intensely through the meadow before its spring was diverted into the reservoir pond that fed our garden. He planted walnut trees that now blaze yellow in October and are the territory of lazuli buntings and black-headed grosbeaks. Beside those trees, the foundation of Bill Graiff's cabin was still visible, but we seldom visited, as if it were a grave with strange undercurrents. Whenever I walked past, I would pause and stare. It was simply a hole of grass and bramble, with evidence of his rock-and-clay cellar, of stones held. I imagined him, tall and lean, ducking under the beams to retrieve a jug of homemade applejack. The orchard was bait. Graiff jarred bear meat and shelved it in his cellar, hibernating the whole animal in pieces.

In the end, this hole was all homesteads, all homesteaders. At the age of eighty-two, Bill Graiff fell out of an apple tree and broke his hip and pelvis. He managed to crawl back into his house and find a white sheet to signal to the bush pilot that flew groceries into the canyon, but he couldn't make it back outside. The pilot found him anyway, still alive, on his regular delivery. Likely he had lain there for days suffering from exposure. He shortly died of pneumonia in town. Dutch Henry's bones, meanwhile, were said to be planted somewhere in the meadow. Undoubtedly we walked over him.

When the Boydens bought the homestead, the timber around the meadow was sold separately and selectively logged. In and of itself, in 1968, it was worth about a million dollars. The true gold, we now know, towered over those early miners. During and after the rush, trees along the coast became San Francisco. Along the Rogue, it wasn't only this modest acreage that had been harvested. To reach the homestead, you circumvented steep recovering clear-cuts, a uniformity of waist-high trees, and from the upper cabin's porch you could see patches on the rumpled blanket thrown to the horizon of the Siskiyous.

From the meadow, ghost logging spurs ran into the forest like veins from a central stem. These were the Caterpillar tracks where fir had been loaded and hauled out. Some were indistinct now, overgrown with saplings, but others were nearly drivable. We explored them at a stroll, brushing the spiders' silk away from our faces. In the fall, some of these dead ends harbored chanterelle mushrooms, which so often thrive on disturbance. Which means, I suppose, that they weren't dead ends, but temporary and fertile earthworks.

That the woods were recovering was a necessary dose of reality for us residents. Here was a haven, a retreat, though once it had been exploited, once it had been worked. Now the forest was working. More than eighty feet tall, as if in retaliation the trees had sawed into the vista of Big Windy from the upper cabin. Time was, said Bradley, from the porch you could see the Rogue pouring like molten iron into Horseshoe Bend, with a gin and tonic in your hand. In another generation, however, a human generation, this one unhinged jaw would clamp down on the mountains entirely. The Boydens weren't allowed to cut trees anymore. They could only hope for a selective wind.

Of all the chores, the largest and most meditative was pulling saplings. This most definitely was allowed and encouraged. We were to pull them along the road's shoulders from the upper gate to the cabins, along the meadow, along the trails—miles of forest edge. We were in the opposite image of Johnny Appleseed. We were reapers of young fir. The Boydens had enlisted us to delay inevitable regrowth and, in this way, we acted like flame.

Most of the saplings were fir, but we pulled tan oak, too—anything that looked as if it might chase the light and soon surpass us. Most came up easy. Sarah prowled one side, I the other. We'd walk slowly, focused, each of us carrying a rusted shovel for the sizable ones that some other, most-negligent and -lazy resident had overlooked. Mainly, though, we used our shovels as walking sticks; I can still hear the stifled clang of our metal tips as we plodded uphill toward the locked gates.

Like mushrooms, saplings begin to "pop out" at you after a while and become a pattern that's easily recognizable. Soon I could spot the jagged ovals of oak and those coniferous bottlebrushes from twenty feet off. Aside from a few excursions for berries or chanterelle in the fall, this chore felt the closest we came to serious foraging. We were picking up acorns, a year too late. Then we'd cast them into the woods like rubbish.

Pulling fir, sometimes I would imagine my hand wrapping around a full-grown tree. I was reaching across the meadow from the porch, tinkering with view. You could feel the rootlets relinquish and hear, or at least imagine, the subtle pop. The carrots in the garden made a louder protest. I uprooted thousands of trees, and now wish I'd thought to collect them all in one place to see the volume, the aspiring forest we held.

Boom. It was afternoon, and it was a crackling boom, like a cannon shot tearing through the timber. It was the kind of boom that should have raised starlings had there been any to speak of in the remote Rogue Canyon. Sarah and I turned and looked at each other. That was a big one, we said. That was one that might always echo in memory.

I found the culprit and the body off the Corral Trail: a legacy Doug fir, one of the largest around, with a trunk six or seven feet in diameter. One of the granddaddies we had admired, with hanging gardens for limbs. It had convulsed downhill and made a clearing for its saplings. The upper trunk lay disarticulated like the spine of a deer carcass, and, scrambling up, I walked and then hopped its length wondering if I might discover bird nests. The trunk was the only clear path. The surroundings were an impassable mess of splinter and needle. The smell, a Christmas tree lot. This was the size of the firs that had stood around the meadow until the sixties, that are still cut daily across the Northwest. The lumber in this tree was a house in and of itself.

Another afternoon, as I was returning to the cabin from the Rogue, I ran into Sarah striding down the trail. Her eyes were wide, her face flush and shaken. She couldn't wait to tell me, so she had taken off downhill: A mammoth snag, a skeletal fir, had fallen directly beside the cabin, but spared it and her. In retrospect, this bleached mast was one of several danger trees behind the cabin; we should have known after we watched two pileated woodpeckers, crow-sized and mockish, at work there one morning, chipping away. Their red crests are both an attractant and a warning. Had that tree fallen twenty feet to the right, this would be another story, so strange to me.

Later I bucked up the downhill portion of this tree, the crown, with the aid of an adventurous friend, Dave, who kayaked the river from Grave Creek to visit us. Red ants poured out one rotted section and ran across our paused blade. We wheelbarrowed the uninfested rounds to level ground near the woodshed. As Red Keller said about a cabin site, "What you need is a good big dead snag you can fall." But not too close.

We were to replace all the firewood we consumed, and in the fall we used our share. The cabin was lightly insulated, the woodstove a comforting hum. Fir and pine sizzled and popped with pitch, and translated more smoke, while fine-grained madrone and oak burned clean and swift. One afternoon, I spotted a fresh madrone just off the driveway and threw on my protective chaps. There may have been more convenient trees to saw, but this girthy madrone, its carnal interior, fixed itself in my mind; I am not a woodsman, but if I were, aesthetics would sway me, as I'm sure it does for many. Sarah helped me carry the rounds to the Jeep, and I could feel all those circular years, that healthy Oregon rain, in my own spine. All those red berries and band-tailed pigeons in the rafters. Bradley had told us that you lift a whole tree seven times from forest to fireplace, something to think about as our logs counted the days.

We left this deciduous redwood to dry in the early fall sun; to cure, as if it were a hock of meat. Later, I spent hours splitting, gradually becoming a more precise and confident shot with the steel maul. Early on, I often would miss my mark, but then metal on metal—maul on wedge—became the rhythm. You have to tighten your arc before letting it out again. Self-control is strength. Gradually, the shed began to refill. These new billets would house mice and lizards. They would warm next year's resident, and then he or she would have to decide which trees to haul and give to others. I drove the wedge into the rounds, and when the ring and split was clean, it was as satisfying as knowing just the right way to finish a paragraph.

We used and split no more than several modest trees; we had no plans to face the winter. But it became clear that what we pulled up in our hands, fresh from its papery husk, and what had made the Rogue woods and air quake, for an instant, and had nearly knifed through the cabin onto Sarah, was also what warmed us and boiled our tea. This tension is what housed us. It encapsulated the homestead. The paradox of fire we came to understand similarly: Fire had provided the meadow and, eventually, it would reclaim it for an afternoon and extend its boundaries, maybe for miles. The very thing that made our life here worrisome also made it possible and worth living.

It was only after the Rogue Wars that the first homesteaders moved into the canyon. Individual miners like Dutch Henry or teams of them traveled west of Grave Creek and built ephemeral cabins in the perennial shade along the river, but our stretch, the upstream end of the canyon, is especially ravined and, for a while, would remain the territory of miners. The earliest homesteaders settled twenty-five miles downstream of us, where today the Rogue River Trail finishes.

They came from California, from the Klamath River just over the border. They were "mixed" couples in the vernacular of the time, unions between miners and Karuk women. Marriages born out of necessity, but often dying in respect and even love, from what I've read. These were the Billingses and the Frys, names that now dominate the middle Rogue. John Billings left Missouri for California and, like Dutch Henry, mined and packed supplies. In 1861, he paid a Karuk woman gold and mules for her daughter, Krum-ket-tika, "flower growing in any place." Her father had been killed by early miners, and afterward she and her mother drifted up the Klamath to a Karuk village in what is today the town of Happy Camp, where her chin was tattooed black with an obsidian blade. John Billings renamed her Adeline. He was thirty-five, she nineteen. Those miners who planned to stay in the hills desired wives; dislocated Native women needed security. Less than ten years after the gold rush's initial violence, some enemies began to knit together.

After seven years of marriage, John and Adeline decided to try the Rogue. Gold had grown scarcer on the Klamath and, as miners left, the pack business dwindled as well. The Billingses made the journey with James and Abraham Fry, who likewise had Karuk wives. For a month, their party broke trail and linked others together: north up Indian Creek and into Oregon, two years before statehood; west across the Smith River, then north again across the Chetco. They settled at the confluence of the Rogue and its largest tributary, the Illinois River. This would be home. John and Adeline tidied an abandoned miner's cabin. She wove a net, and they caught and dried enough salmon to last the winter.

The Billingses didn't have claim to this land, however, so they moved upriver, finally settling for good at Big Meadows, the counterpart to our Little ones, which are five miles farther upstream. In 1888, they earned title to 320 acres, where they built a log cabin. John tried to run sheep on his homestead, but he lost them to predators. "He used to tell about how he tried to kill them coyotes," one friend, Leo Frye, remembered in *Illahe*. "He said they were smarter than he was." John would bury three eggs, one filled with the poison found in nightshade. But Coyote—or *pihne-fic*, as Adeline called him in Karuk—would eat two and leave the dud for John.

Apparently John didn't have much of a sense of humor. "A bear's sweet-natured alongside of him," another neighbor recalled. But he was respected. "He was just a good old man," Leo Frye maintained. "His family never went hungry for anything." Adeline outlived him, her whole life making traditional baskets from hazel root that she sold or gifted. She also bore ten children.

From the Curry County probate records, the names of John Billings's mules and horse:

Jim Mule	*16 years old*
Flossie Mare	*14 years old*
Jermie Mule	*12 years old*
Pete Mule	*10 years old*
Jack Mule	*10 years old*

Johnnie Mule	*8 years old*
Cy Mule	*8 years old*
Hussie Mule	*7 years old*
Pearly Mule	*4 years old*
Millie Mule	*3 years old*

Always the day is ahead or behind in a forest, as if night both recedes into and emerges from trees, gathering above hollow trunks the way swifts gather to roost. As Bradley had told us, during that last hour we could keep time by the orange climbing Rattlesnake Ridge. Down at the river, I'd linger, wait until that line of rising alpenglow was all but gone, before hitting the trail, where the gloam was easy, refreshing, broken sometimes by shades of salmon through the trees overhead. I'd turn my fly rod around in my hand and let the tip follow me home, so as not to lance it into the ground or tangle with the trees.

Crossing our home creek one evening, I saw the shape of a bat swoop and graze the water, leaving a ripple, and I thought of the water strider alive in its mouth, those thread-thin legs splayed across its gums. Occasionally a deer would startle and bound away through the drowned branches. Rarely, at dusk, we heard a saw-whet owl, as if a lumberjack was still out there, intent on felling a tree the old-fashioned way. Otherwise there was only the almost-silence of scattered birds, of chickadees and vireos. If the trees weren't roaring.

The meadow announced itself from a few hundred feet out: the expanse always bright, even late. Twilight clings to grass. First, the black oak below the barn twisted into my view; then the slumping pole-and-shake barn, which, especially at this hour, would make a Rogue hiker imagine he'd stumbled onto a miner's acre; and finally the *A* of the lower cabin, its one solar panel and sliding glass door reflecting the empty ceiling over Rattlesnake Ridge. And inside, Sarah.

Then the meadow was a black lake. For weeks, at night we heard an anonymous shriek, brief and high-pitched. I wondered: Other residents had seen cougar at the homestead, and later in the season I would find the lobed impressions of a mother and her cub in the damp sand along the river. Several times, I stood on the porch with a flashlight trying to spotlight the sound, my shadow thrown long across the meadow like a fallen tree. Finally I beamed the fox, silvery and embered on the road, and that particular mystery flickered and went out. But it never could entirely.

As soon as we turned on a lamp in the cabin, we were shut in. The Rogue swallowed us so completely we didn't know it was there. We were in a forested crevasse, a crevice of the world. In addition to those LED lights, the cabin was lit by propane lanterns, copper wire snaking to globes above the sinks, the kitchen table, the couch, and our bed. Push the lever in and down and you would hear the hiss. We set the lighter's flame under the wicket's ash hive, which gave form to those exploding molecules. Where the gas had come from besides our robin's egg tank and Grants Pass, I don't know.

"For light I was usin' a cake of grease," Red Keller said. "Take a piece of string, and wrap it around, put a piece of bailin' wire over it to make a groove, and that knot in there works just like a candle. You just light that and the wick will draw the grease up. You can use bear grease, but I never monkeyed around much with bear unless I just had to." I can't quite picture how Red rigged his grease from these words, but I imagine his gestures, his sure hands.

If we touched the cold wicket of a lamp, it crumbled and sifted to the floor or the seam of our palms, just ash. Several times a moth careered into a lit one to their mutual demise. They were expensive, ten or fifteen dollars each. Bradley had cautioned us to handle them carefully. Whenever one broke, I would set another in its base like a thief, making sure it hung level and firm. Then we would kindle the new, stiff basket until it caught, and watch the orange line crawl and smoke up its side. It needed to be burned before it was ready for use, and afterward it was more fragile than a spiderweb.

Mice run as wires: along and through walls. They are as electric in their obscurity. They seem to recognize a cabin no matter how far it is from town. Part of me had imagined them aloof in the meadow, felling one stalk of grass at time for the seed like little lumberjacks, but they preferred our Tostitos shards. I remember dropping to my knees once to look under our half-sized oven with a flashlight and discover the hulking shape of an avocado pit—and a mouse, the same size and brown, twitching behind in the cobwebs. But more often we would only sense movement.

One mouse we heard make a trail: behind the couch, past the sliding porch doors, into the corner to explore, over and over, the box of recycling underneath the sink. A solitary clink, a vitreous or aluminum scurry. But we did nothing. We had rinsed each can; the mouse would soon have nothing to lick. The sound was almost reassuring: At least someone around here was being productive tonight. I don't mind a mouse, but you wouldn't want two shacking up in a love grove under your watch. Bradley had told us to poison them with the cartons of pellets in the shed, and eventually we set one out. Which I regret, since that poison then runs out the door into the clutches of owls. A clean snap is more upstanding, if you have to.

Sitting in the rocker one evening, I heard a whispering in the rusted smoker that sat in the porch's corner beside the specimen table. With a flashlight, Sarah and I peered through one of its vents and, there, on an enormous mattress woven of our couch's stuffing, a petite mouse was settled with cool blue sparks for eyes. This mouse, we realized, was squeezing through a gap between the screen door and its frame. We laughed and fawned over it as we poured light through its steel window. It had built its home in a bundle of apple-branch kindling.

Every few weeks, we drove to Grants Pass for errands, and sometimes to discover monumental news like the death of Michael Jackson. We took the recycling with us and carried it rattling into Safeway's recycling annex. You can deposit your bottles and cans for five cents a pop and receive a coupon for redemption inside the store. One day, at the bottom of our modest box, inside an hourglass salsa jar, we found a madcap cache of lime-green pellets: a winter's larder of poison.

The first time a bear hit the fence in the dark, I thought of a certain well-known dinosaur movie. All was lost, clearly, all those runty vegetables. The metal rattled fiercely amid grunts not out of proportion with the darkness of the Rogue. From the porch, I swept a thousand-candle flashlight through the garden, searching the barbwire perimeter and the leaning trees clear across the meadow as if from a tower.

In the morning, we assessed the damage: The far side of the garden fence sagged like the idle, half-strung guitar I had brought to the homestead hoping to learn. The electric wire was pulled from its runners. The fence we'd so diligently pounded into the ground had been yanked hard, so that little peaks of wire, handfuls, rose like waves. But it held. No bear ever barged in, so far as we know. I think the fox walked right in, though, and pilfered our dwarf cantaloupe to make sweet milk for her kits.

When Bradley was fourteen, he and his mother arrived at the Horseshoe Bend cabin one summer to find a bear had beaten them there and had a "good thrash," to employ one of Bradley's favorite phrases. It had strewn things about, dug into the flour and left ghostly muzzle and paw prints across the walls. So Red Keller hung a side of bacon from a nearby tree and set the jaws in the leaves. In the night, the canyon was summoned by that inhuman bawling, and Bradley was recruited to end it. He aimed Red's gun at that moving misfortune, that burly spotlit figure, and pulled the trigger. But another man on hand fired the kill shot.

"I always had a dog for the bear," Red Keller said. "Three years straight I had bears break into my cabin. One year they cleaned me clear out of groceries. Broke right through the windows. I got each bear. They'll just tear everything up." Those words stay with me: *I got each bear.* Maybe Red Keller did get them in another sense as well, understood them as they can be, as animals that live a solitary life of abiding hunger. He shot or trapped them when they forced his hand, and only ate them when he joined Bill Graiff at the homestead for dinner. It was better Graiff's way, Red Keller said: boiled and canned.

The upper cabin had a swath of bright tan shingles above the porch, where a wall had been patched; where one winter, a bear tried to tear through. When they arrived in the spring, Bradley and Frank discovered what was so irresistible: a can of smoked oysters. It had rusted through and leaked into the boards. The Boydens hired a trapper to capture that troublemaker and, in this age, simply relocate it. The trapper trucked in a steel cage on a trailer and parked it on the road near the upper cabin. Inside, on the trip lever, he placed a single mini marshmallow and scattered a few more. They got that bear.

I began to feel guilty about keeping the bears out of the garden, because by September it was a glut of apples, most of which we let rot. We could consume only so many in Sarah's pies, and we didn't have the wherewithal, the mindfulness, to can them, or we might be eating them still. Now that drives home how little she and I were actually homesteading; makes it clear that life in the woods, with a car and no intention of wintering, is not exactly life in the woods.

Old-timers in the Rogue Canyon went so far as to jar their game. "You could hunt deer in the winter and can it," said Red Keller. "You have jars and just boil it. You bone it, cut it, and pack it in the jars. Put your lids on and let it come to a boil. Just so it's boilin' for three hours. Then it's done and it'll keep forever." "I like cooking for myself," he added. The Takelma and Shasta Costa dried salmon and venison, cached acorns and camas flour. Dutch Henry spent days mule-packing his apples over the drainages to market, on the road we drove impatiently in an hour and a half. We never even bothered to make apple butter. We relied on Safeway's bounty.

But some of the apples we sliced and lay on the screen trays of the dehydrator. It was located in the middle of the garden, to avoid trouble, a freestanding cupboard with a glass ceiling slanted to the south. Each time I unlatched its door, a blue-bellied western fence lizard would scurry out on its long-nailed toes, or along the box's edge—such a warm, aromatic home. Though I later found one, maybe the same, withered like dried fruit on the dehydrator's floor. We filled empty half-gallon nut containers with gummy rings and ate them by the handful until they molded.

One tree in the garden was so bowed with apples that finally several branches snapped, and we felt like terrible caretakers for having failed to prop them up with the fir poles that littered the woods. We had slung a hammock in this garden grove, which added a welcome stroke of artificial color to the view; Sarah made a painting of it, a crescent of red and blue in the dapple. I remember lying in the hammock in late August as the bees and yellow jackets cruised the bruised and melting spoils below, their drone filling me, my ears. They prodded the craters in these golden planets, all tumbled together in a mass extinction, and carried samples to their underground colonies.

Another day I discovered a mouse dead on the road between the cabins. Hard to say what killed it—not a car, and we hadn't stepped on it. We wondered if this was our friend from the porch's smoker, who had disappeared. It was a body untouched, still plump with water. Then the yellow jackets arrived, one by one, and began to saw, peeling the fur, taking the inner wreckage away piecemeal to a nest, some old burrow along the edges of the meadow lined with papery walls. Eventually the mouse was reduced to a husk. In this way, it was demonstrated that the difference between a mouse and an apple is minimal.

We found the yellow jackets' nest only as we pulled saplings one afternoon beyond the garden, just where a dead snag had fallen, given in, to the meadow. Sarah found it, rather. Suddenly she shrieked and threw her shovel aside and her hands up in the hot air as she leaped sideways through the grass. There were jackets swirling around her, and at least one was trapped in her clothes. "Take your shirt off!" I yelled, several times. She was modest even alone in the woods, miles from anyone. Finally she stood there in her purple bra, cringing and sobbing a little, her shovel in the grass. I rubbed her shoulders. This was their home, too, their field.

Now I wonder if it was poison they had whisked away.

Sarah and I often would make a simple dinner of couscous and pork chop with sautéed garden apples and carry it in old yogurt containers, along with a couple of beers, to the upper cabin's porch, where the view was to Big Windy. We'd unlock the front door and slip through the stale and dusty air, listening to the bats quivering in the walls as the afternoon sun turned their roost behind the shingles into a hothouse. Then out the sliding glass door. We'd unfold the plastic chairs leaned against the walls. Having one porch was deeply satisfying; having another for our use with such an expansive, undulating prospect was an utter luxury we tried not to waste. The light climbing Rattlesnake Ridge was a dying wildfire that never died.

In August, the bears finally came out of the Rogue's green curtain and went up into Dutch Henry's doddering apple trees, such broken figures, especially after the bears. More than once, a mother and two cubs emerged—one black, the other cinnamon—and climbed as a family. She was teaching them local conveniences; these cubs would teach theirs as future residents looked on. Another evening, a large male, the biggest bear we saw, swaggered through the ferns as we held our forks in the air, and he rose up on his hind legs to shake each tree, with his pale gray testicles hanging low. He was so big he didn't need to climb. His reach was enough.

If there were no bears below the upper cabin, there were deer. They would walk cautiously, on stilts, from the tan oaks, pausing every few steps in case of an audience. But on the porch, we were behind a curtain, somehow. We were deck furniture. Come fall, the bucks emerged with blood-velvet peeling from their antlers like bark from madrone. They honed their points on Dutch Henry's orchard trees, and later racked them against each other, though more often feuds were settled with a brief, ritualized chase, the dominant buck on the heels of the upstart. Then they harassed the does, who trotted off, wanting only grass.

Red Keller described his way of fishing, the preferred method for rainbows up the Rogue's tributary creeks: "Take a willow pole and put a line on it. Take a leader and use a piece of bacon for bait. Down there in lots of places you can't get worms. You pull the eye out of the first one you catch and use that. They'll like it because it shines."

We would lash a wet fly, a one-inch streamer, into the Rogue and, inexplicably, sometimes a half-pounder would scintillate and hit it. Then the game of telephone: The only time you feel the whole life force of a fish is before you finally wrap your hands around its exhausted body; the only time is through synthetic twine. A half-pounder is a steelhead, or an oceangoing trout, that has returned to its natal river after less than a year in the Pacific, when normally they spend several, growing to eight or ten pounds before running home to breed. No one knows why, exactly. But these were strong for their size, and sometimes I would let them run out again, just to continue to feel their energy. When they disappeared, dove into the blackness, it was as if I had the river.

Often I would have to climb down from a boulder, sometimes a fair ways, to land a fish. I would dip my hand in anticipation and study the lithe steelhead as it approached to see if it had a clipped fin. If so, it was a hatchery fish. I must have caught thirty or so half-pounders that fall, and only two were wild. Which isn't a good sign, though probably wild fish are savvier. But all of them had beaten the odds and explored the ocean, and now as then, I'm not convinced that being conceived in a steel tank makes it any less so.

Some of those clipped half-pounders I let free. Others I would withdraw like a sword and thwack on the stone so that I could feel and hear the crack of the skull: any memory, the intuition of life in water—of the Pacific—rattled and gone. It was the last season, for now, that I would kill a fish. Sometimes I cleaned them there on the riverbank with my Swiss Army knife, turning the tip inside its stomach to unseal and scrape the bloodline, and left the viscera for the water. Their flesh was a gentle pink, partway to salmon, a sign of the sea, of great clouds of krill. I'd drag them to rinse the cavity. One last swim.

We grilled the fish on the porch in our Weber, laying fresh apple twigs on the coals for the tartness of smoke. Head and all, in the skin. Their eyes metamorphosed to quartz. It felt right to eat something that we had caught and to an extent lived with. Fish bones near the cabin or in the compost would never do, on account of the bears, so we wrapped the remainders in plastic and, the next time we were in Grants Pass, covertly dumped them with all the rest of our trash into a random dumpster. That's one way to deal with your waste when you reside in the backcountry. But if I were to do it all over again, I'd bring each fish back to the river.

In the height of summer, we camped by the Rogue on just a tarp and pads, but later in the fall, with mist in the air, we pitched a dome tent on Horseshoe Bar, the leading edge of Horseshoe Bend. Sarah stayed to read or paint while I fished the curve, where I had caught a number of half-pounders. I had been so bold as to suggest that we might roast one on a river-tooth fire. But taking a step to reposition myself, I misjudged an angle on a slick rock and fell backward, straight back. As I went, I understood my head was unprotected and my skull was about to crack on the sable stone, and the lights would go out.

My arms flung down and back with the rod still in my hand. My backside slammed, and I heard and felt the sharp metallic of the reel striking rock. I stared at the sky where I fell: a marine layer marbled with seams. The wind had been knocked out of my canyon; I felt dizzy, nauseous, gut-punched. But after a minute, it passed. My head was fine. Only my shoulder and gluteus maximus were bruised and beginning to tighten. I rolled off the rock into a wet triangle of sand with willow shoots and knelt there, hands on my thighs, contemplating these results. Seemed fair. I gave up the evening and limped home, to the cobble. My butt cheek turned the color of crushed blackberries, then the yellow and brown of an apple mushed on the ground.

I remember reading one evening on the upper cabin's porch from Hayden Carruth's *Toward the Distant Islands: New and Selected Poems*. A copy was floating around because Frank Boyden, an artist, had done the cover detail. Inside was an elegy that Carruth wrote for his daughter, Martha, the day after she died of cancer in her forties: "She who became a painter and who now is / the painter forever, / of these images of earthly splendor and fascination / on our walls, / from here to California." He had stayed up all night to write the poem and chronicle the changes of the light out his upstate New York window. I remember reading that aloud to Sarah and having my mouth go dry.

Then water came to our eyes. It wasn't only the beer, but the layered view that was heaviest at certain late, but always changing, moments. It was our isolation, our vulnerable age, our firm but tenuous hold on each other. Looking out, with these words in the air, we sensed that. We sensed that it could only ever be. In "Dearest M—", Carruth describes a deer under an apple tree rising up on her hind legs to grasp an apple with her teeth. "But she cannot." We'd seen them do exactly this, and manage it, from the porch. Their forelegs lift to their chests and their hooves dangle as if vestigial. They look like different animals entirely.

We felt then a small wave, call it sadness. It was about what all people know so intensely as those they love or know disappear, which could include a place or time. It felt as bright as the orange crawling up Rattlesnake Ridge. Most days, this landscape was a playground, an inspiration to us. But an apple tree can just as easily be a somber form, a broken hip. It can signal a lost homeland. It can be all these things, and it can also be a way forward. Lou Martin, another miner on the Rogue, had come from Maine, as far as the continent would allow, following the flu epidemic of 1918: "After my wife and baby died, I went into the hills. I don't know how to express it. I can put it this way. If you're busy, if you are working, your mind is occupied and you don't miss the other party. That's the way it is in the hills. Most of the fellows that stayed in the hills felt the same way." That's also what to homestead can mean.

When Sarah's parents arrived for a visit in September, their first time in Oregon, we tapped nails lightly into some of the love grove's trees and hung a selection of her paintings for a one-day-only gallery, a plein air surprise. She needed no other structure, no track lighting or frames. To a fir, I stapled an announcement of the retrospective; weeks later, that paper would melt off the tree in the rain. At the opening, we opened the beer cache to find Solo cups and a bottle of chardonnay, chilled by the Rogue earth. The show was trees on trees, the way the world still is in many places, trees on trees without misgiving. As it should be. Fallen giants become "nurse logs," giving their nutrients, all of them, to the feathery saplings that grow off their backs.

We walked around the grove with our hands on our hips and admired her foliation of color, how she'd managed so cleanly to show the messiness of the meadow's border. This was Sarah's love, its full expression, though she felt she hadn't fully expressed it. She had slung the hammock red-and-blue in the garden. She had entwined maple and the dim of the creek. There were deer in her paintings, some below the apple trees, grazing or watchful, their ears cocked. The deer walked through our lives so much that we began to forget them and seeing them on her canvases was a reminder. They were there. They watched us.

My own parents brought the dogs: a handsome mutt, Dama, rescued from New Orleans, sleek and tawny as a young mountain lion; and two chihuahuas, surprising hikers, but ridiculous in the backcountry. No match for a lion or a squirrel. We trekked to Kelsey Creek and left the heat in the runoff still gathering from snow that, most years, keeps people out of the homestead by car until May. When one of the chihuahuas fell in, she paddled like a merganser to the bank with furious eyes. Meanwhile, Dama raced ahead and behind on trails of air, as she always does, bothering the chipmunks. As we lingered by Kelsey, she emerged from the brush with a long, straight bone. We joked nervously that it might be human, some victim of the Rogue Wars. Probably it was a deer femur.

On the way back, Dama found another treasure. "Come here, Dama, what do you have?" I stopped her on the trail, pulled it from her warm and dripping gums: It was two shriveled fingers, still connected. A half-curled fragment of a hand. We gaped; there seemed no point in recoiling from what was impossible. Here were the missing digits of Mr. William Black more than a century later. Here was evidence of a humanlike creature unknown to us. But they appeared, in fact, to be a desiccated bear paw, just as queer and grisly: long claws, coarse sooty bristles, the cured and peeling skin of a hairless pad.

I carried this relic home in my own right hand and left it on the porch table, beside the weathered dictionary and the lifeless hummingbird, the beaver skull and the .22 shells, the ponderosa cone and a river tooth. This was something all residents should examine, and I wonder, now, if it is still there to see. All summer and fall that dilapidated plywood table gathered our experience, like an eddy. Some of it. It was an open-air curiosity cabinet that allowed us to hold the landscape we had found, to remember its many inhabitants and habitats, even if it was only a partial distillation, an impoverished theater of the Rogue. It was easy, for me, to gather natural history, more difficult to conjure the human.

We celebrated Sarah's twenty-fifth birthday the night before she left. Bradley and Lang, the homestead's second resident—the intrepid mountain biker who had survived and named Rattlesnake Ridge—drove in for their annual fall visit, the homestead's closure. But I was staying on; I was eager to try a month of solitude, and Sarah was happy to go back east and join her family for the holidays, to give me that experiment. She would pilot the Jeep to the Bay Area with our stuff, and in a month, I would walk out of the Rogue on the trail with what I could carry. The pass might be snowbound.

We grilled that night at the upper cabin, and I mixed up a Funfetti cake, Sarah's request. We drank Bradley's whiskey and lost at cribbage. The next afternoon, she and I drove out behind them. They turned for Portland, and we spent one last night in Grants Pass in our grand and plain motel, the Knights Inn, where we had stayed several times: for a Halloween out on the town, and when we had too many errands. I stayed up far too late revising an essay on sudden notice so I could send it off and then slid into bed beside her. The next morning, she dropped me back off at Grave Creek, and I started up the rocky stretch before the trail turns out of sight, where I waved and blew a kiss.

The Rogue River Trail runs forty miles, but I was going only fifteen. She and I had hiked it midsummer, camping one night on a sandbar, on a blue crinkled tarp, but now I walked it in five hours, stepping over the river's tributaries, sometimes on wooden bridges: After Grave Creek came China Gulch, where a team of Chinese miners, whom we tend to forget, had toiled before the turn of the century. Then Whiskey Creek, Rum Creek, Doe Creek. Alder and Booze, Hayward and Bronco. Big Windy, Bunker, Little Windy, Jenny, Copsey, Cowley, and Meadow. Each with a sordid or sad or simple story that's mostly washed out with the gold and the rain.

Later in his life, Red Keller preferred winters in the canyon, when the steelhead were running and the rafters weren't. Mere visitors like us were a distraction. "When you're down that way you'll read an awful lot," said Red. "I wouldn't live in town. Just nothin' for me to do. There I can be just as happy running along the river and foolin' around. Lookin' out the window when it's snowin' hard, read a little bit, wonder how long it's going to last, and how deep it is. Then first thing in the morning, I get up and take off and see the different fresh tracks in the snow." During my month alone, flakes the size of feathers shrouded the meadow just once. Gone by afternoon.

But another morning the meadow began as an unexpected porcelain, a frost so complete that each stalk of grass lay thickly glazed. It was the kind of frost that, when you see it, seems to send fractals into your lungs and suppress your breath without notice or discomfort. No sound. I stepped onto the porch, into this transformation. The night before, the meadow had been in fog, and it had left another version of itself. Walking up the road, the spiderwebs sagged in lucid imperfection, like the garden fence after the bear. They would snap back to shape only as they became invisible. The meadow again dripped to normal by midday, and it pained me that no one else, especially Sarah, had seen it.

Darkness entered the forest early that last month, though I hadn't reset my watch with the end of daylight savings. No need. I did read many hours on the cinnamon couch, as much as I ever had: Willa Cather's *O Pioneers!*, Ken Kesey's *One Flew Over the Cuckoo's Nest*, Jack Kerouac's *Desolation Angels*, Wallace Stegner's *Angle of Repose*, Ernest Hemingway's *For Whom the Bell Tolls*. I remember reading *As I Lay Dying* for the first time, in the murmuring company of the woodstove, and reimagining those saw-whet owls we had heard as Cash Bundren prepared to bevel his mother's final home, while she listened from her sickbed through their cabin window. Faulkner, it turns out, visited the Rogue in the 1940s.

It was a tradition for each resident to leave at least one recommended read on the cabin's three-shelf library, and I donated a few: Lewis Hyde's *The Gift*, on the creative spirit, which my sister had given to me and in which I first read about the Northwest's tribal salmon ceremonies, how the bones and skin of a sacred fish are returned to the river to ensure they will come again. And a how-to-prospect-for-gold book, in which I inscribed an inspirational note and cheekily taped a flake of gold, a small one I had panned out of the river (the others I kept). Some residents had left the books they had written, and I imagined someday returning to put mine on the shelf for others to browse or use as a coaster on the porch. These were the quiet days of December.

In Sarah's absence, I took a few more ambitious hikes to pass the time and see farther corners. There was Zane Grey's fishing cabin to finally visit, just past Battle Bar. The log house was locked, but I pressed my nose to the wavering glass and, nearby, found elk tracks and pellets in the vigorous winter grass. And on another cloudless morning in December, I started for the top of Rattlesnake Ridge. We had stared at its raw face so much I had to climb.

From the Corral, I headed up-meadow until the grass tapered to a forested ridge choked with brush—manzanita, in particular, is unforgiving. Eventually I bushwhacked to a forgotten logging spur that connected with the jeep trail on Rattlesnake's spine. I expected to see no snakes this time of year; they would be in their collective dens, their hibernacula, in torpor. But I was on guard anyway.

Where the road gave out, I remember sitting on a ledge beside a large, wind-bitten tree and peering straight down on the Bend, which, for the first time, was plainly a horseshoe. I wore it on my battered feet. Crows played below me, their shadows miming against the talus below the ridge, which in this spot was every bit the wall it looked from our porch. If I fell, my eyes would invite the hooked bill of the corvid.

I ate my peanut butter sandwich. The river was a shiver, a runnel that deflected off the canyon wall beyond our home creek and turned out of sight, disappearing but never gone toward Kelsey. This described the territory I'd come to know. I could see the Little Meadows, the Corral and ours, those handprints of fire. The *A* of the lower cabin and the mowed garden. The apple trees below the porch and Bill Graiff's walnuts, now free of their fall saffron. I tried to memorize the view, which from this height seemed untouched by all the people that had flowed through.

Then I plunged down the Rattlesnake, glissading through scales of scree and fragile earth; catching trees with my hands and swinging myself around to temper my fall, my momentum, as if I were planting poles on a ski slope. Giving in to gravity, you're less likely to turn an ankle. Lower, I wove though huckleberry taller than me, shouting, "You, bear!" though the fruit was gone, until I hit the bank of the

Rogue River Trail. I remembered that Sarah and I had picked berries just here and boiled exactly two eight-ounce jars of purple jam to give to our families at Christmas.

For a moment, the soft, level ground of the trail was foreign and anticlimactic. Then it began to feel good. The whole month I saw no one along the river.

There was a cold spell, cold for southern Oregon. Two or three nights the temperatures fell to the low twenties or high teens. I hunkered down with the woodstove, digging out the coals in the ash as soon as I pulled off the bedcovers. "At Horseshoe Bend I had a cook stove," Red Keller said. "You couldn't keep that cabin warm, but I got used to it. Anybody come to see me called it the 'deep freeze.' I had it one time with the fire going all night and the next morning there was a lot of ice in the bucket of water." With the sun of early afternoon, the temperature rose a fair ways above freezing, but it was expected to dive again.

I was reading, when suddenly there was a terrific hissing beneath me. I put on my shoes and ran outside. Under the cabin, water was jetting from a pipe that clearly had frozen, burst, and now thawed. Aside from a sporadic wrap of foam insulation, the plumbing was exposed below the floorboards. I had known that I needed to keep water moving in the severe cold, so I'd left the faucets dripping in the sinks. But the pitter hadn't been enough.

This time, I thought, the bear's jumped on my back: If I don't fix the leak and get the system flowing in an hour, other sections of pipe will freeze and burst at sundown. I could drain the cabin, but then I wouldn't be able to stoke the fire. The charcoal-encrusted pipes that coiled through the stove to produce hot water would melt if they were left empty. The stove would be ruined.

Briskly I walked to the upper cabin's toolshed and rummaged for the blowtorch and solder wire. In June, Bradley had showed us how, but now it was December and I had no notes. My memory is often short; mostly I'm suited for meadow-watching. But with a handsaw, I cut out the split section, about four inches of pipe. Two fittings, copper bands, would join a new, shiny length of pipe to these sawed ends. With sandpaper, I wrung the cut edges to smooth them, inside and out, and to subtly score the metal, which would allow solder to flow down a thousand microscopic creeks and grip. Then I lit the blowtorch and held a blue pencil of flame.

It wasn't working, and no wonder. Most days I can't spell "solder." Then I looked off into the meadow, dug deep, and channeled Bradley: You don't heat the solder. You heat the joint alone, and then touch the tip of the unspooled solder wire to it. The silver wicked into the seam and circled the joint faster than I could see. Three more seals, and I restored water to the cabin. Putting my ear to the pipe, I heard movement inside, the tiniest of rivers; the eventual Rogue.

Two days before my own twenty-fifth birthday, I left the Rogue. It was an overcast morning in December, a fundamental Oregon day. I was to hike out, without a mule, to meet my father at the Grave Creek trailhead. It had been a mild winter to that point, precipitation-wise, and likely he could have driven the dirt roads over the pass. But that was the arrangement.

In September, Sarah had hung her paintings in the love grove, but what did I have to show for myself? Nothing so visible. I had scattered my time like madrone leaves, which flash an indecisive pale and dark as they twirl and fall: a month writing novice poetry, a month on a few mediocre stories, another editing a literary journal I would soon let unravel, and one more tweaking those Rhode Island essays that really needed wholesale reinvention. It all amounted to splitting rounds for the firewood I would have to later burn for heat. Which I hope means those words were not wasted. You have to spend energy to gather it. You have to homestead, dig in today for future seasons.

All morning, I battened down the property. The garden beds were tilled by hand and again under tarp. The water system was drained, those pipes below the cabin now roaring through open valves to the bare red earth, as they were supposed to. I diced my few remaining vegetables, cucumbers and onions and a pepper, and gave them a turn in the waterlogged compost barrel for the next summer's resident to spread if the bears didn't enjoy the slurry first.

To my dismay and mild panic, however, I ran behind schedule on these final chores and locked the cabin door an hour later than necessary to meet my father so we could make our Medford flight and join my family for the holidays. My pack was forty or fifty pounds. It was fifteen rolling miles upstream to Grave Creek, five hours of walking. I had four. So for a few hours, I jogged the flats and downhills, cinched tight and feeling the Rogue hard in my knees.

The river was alone, full and resonant. My body would be sore for days. I was the only person in the blessed, evergreen canyon. What I remember most was pausing at the top of a rise and unzipping my pack to dump weight. I had a few pounds of chocolate truffles, still in their open package of golden foil, that a friend had kindly sent to our P.O. box in Grants Pass. I ate one more and, with a heave, scattered the rest toward the river, several handfuls down the hillside into the trees. I wondered how many the animals would find.

The poets left their work on the walls: one poem each. They would hold as long as the staples. Sarah hung a painting of a walnut tree and empty bathtub above the radiophone, and though I wasn't at the homestead as a poet, beside the woodstove I tacked up something basic, "September." It was a poem about bushtits, small gray songbirds I grew up with in the oak and chaparral of California. Gregarious, and always in tight flocks of fifteen or twenty. The males with bright gold irises.

I ran into them just once at the homestead as they trailed from the apple trees. They fly haltingly. They have short wings: "One moves," I wrote, "a brief, impromptu space, / moth-like, a mote of dust to a pine bough. / They all follow, as if tied, / save those with the long / lengths, endlessly left behind / and latching on again, as days." To become at home in a place, I think, is mainly to try to discover the words for things. The names. *Bushtit.*

In the meadow, we found potholes where bears had dug yellow jacket nests, perhaps years ago, and sucked the larvae from their nurseries. Apparently a wasp sting is nothing to a bear, which makes me wonder about the effectiveness of our electricity. The shreds of the jacket's wallpaper, gray as newsprint, lay scattered about these excavations, and I would think of those wasps masticating pulp and depositing it underground. I'd imagine that they had, or soon would, steal bits of the dictionary that was disintegrating on the porch aside the beaver skull and paste stray words inside the meadow: *crepuscular, apricity, rogue.*

This whole meadow, I realized, was papered with words, with stories and sketches and histories, and I would add a few. You can build a shelter from words. The poems stapled in the cabin would eventually cover the walls, like the thinnest of cedar shakes, and become a cabin themselves. And when the bear clawed or nuzzled into that house, it would return to the clay of vocabulary, become a madrone, drift again.

Slow Flame

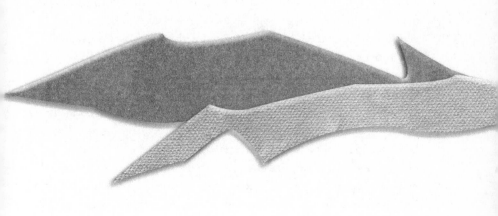

Once, in Northern California, she and I were walking through a redwood park with old-growth trees, when we heard something up a side canyon, a kind of whispering. Curious, we walked up the draw along a deer trail and discovered a wildfire burning unannounced in the forest, a line of flame hardly wider than my hand. It was windless and quiet—not even the sound of wrens—and the fire was moving a few inches at a time. You could stand there and watch it come forward as if it were creeping on its belly, and I remember thinking: Even a newt could outrun this.

There is a canyon next to my old home south of San Francisco, one among many, and as in most canyons, the legacy redwoods were cut a century ago. The enormous stumps remind of wrecked ships. But a few great trees remain higher up, still clinging to the steepest ground, the most difficult to cut. Almost all of them are fire-scarred: their fibrous bark singed, or their hearts fully hollowed and charred. Redwoods survive fires because their wood is saturated with tannins, a fire retardant and also a mild poison, which gives them their sunset interior.

In this forest and the surrounding oak woodlands, during certain times of the year, one can find California newts, *Taricha torosa*, ambling carelessly, it seems, in all directions. They are the color of decaying needle: deep brown on top, their underbellies a brilliant orange. They hatch in cold creeks and ponds, where for a time they have feathery external gills, but they become terrestrial during the late summer, walking off into the duff in search of bloodworms and sow bugs. At the first hard rain, they return to their waters of origin to spawn and, each winter, a few adults returned to our concrete basement, to the flooded drain where they were born.

When threatened by a prodding finger, *Taricha* newts curl their tails over their granular backs in an arch, an act as sensual as it is intimidating. When I was young, I wondered why I never found their bones in the pellets of the great horned owls roosting in the shadows of certain trees, but it's not because they seem to have none: Their skin carries a poison, tetrodotoxin, hundreds of times more potent than cyanide— easily enough to kill a grown human, if you were to swallow one and keep it from wriggling back up into the light. So they flash their golden undersides as if to say, *Wash your hands, wash your hands.* Only garter snakes, with a red stripe down their backs, have evolved immunity. They strangle and gulp newts whole.

Newts belong to the family Salamandridae, and in the occult, the salamander is believed to have a unique connection to fire and, thus, medicinal properties. Aristotle wrote, "And the Salamander shows that it is possible for some animal substances to exist in the fire, for they say fire is extinguished when this animal walks over it." Pliny the Elder concurred: "This animal is so intensely cold as to extinguish fire by its contact, in the same way that ice does." Their glistening skin does suggest an immense wetness. And as newts and salamanders often hide or hibernate in logs, probably they are sometimes found near or among the ashes of a hearth. I have never seen such a thing, but I have found snakeskin in a woodstove, its broad belly scales glowing like windows.

One year our basement flooded during a heavy December storm. My mother enlisted us to help mop up the rain that was seeping in, somehow, through the walls; the same rain that was also feeding a hidden pool, the perennial source of young newts that would stumble inside and wander the concrete. A thick blue carpet was sopping, as heavy as stone and destined for the dumpster, while the skirt of an old couch wicked water toward its cushions. A mop already leaned against one wall, and when I lifted it, newts came tumbling out of the woolly dreadlocks, plopping quietly. But not all of them: We had to shake out others that clung to these coils of moisture like children to a mother's hair.

When they landed squirming on the concrete, they turned over so lazily, almost reluctantly, and returned to their feet. Began to pace. Over the years, I would carry them outside by the handful, most of them first-year newts, about two inches long. As a child, to hold one in your hand is to imagine holding a newborn. Even as an adult. The peculiar softness of it, the pinky quality, their slow motions. Momentarily your hand becomes a womb in which you hold a memory or premonition of your own evolution.

Inevitably I would forget to check the basement and some would desiccate, the moisture run out. In a desk drawer in my former room there is a tiny white jewelry gift box, made of cardboard, that perhaps once belonged to my mother. Inside I gathered the dead like potpourri, this beautiful "rotten" flesh. Through parchment skin, you can see the bracelet of their spines. Only the faintest of smells, something like the apricot scent of the chanterelle slices we dried each winter. I stole them from the basement and shut them up in my cardboard sarcophagus, occasionally lifting the lid to look in. As if to see if they were ready to rise and go, back to the redwoods. *Taricha* in fact means "mummy," their name likely inspired by their warty appearance in life.

I remember one particular year finding newts squashed by the dozen on the road leading to our house. It was just as I became aware of their existence, and mainly I recall feeling helpless to save them, to stand guard long enough. Pressed to the pavement like giant worms, their pygmy limbs and jaws were identifiable among the otherwise freeform S of their bodies. There are particular roads in Northern California that, thankfully, close each year to cars during the newt migration, including one famous stretch in Tilden Park of Berkeley from November through April. Yellow *Newt Crossing* signs—a black, curled silhouette floating at center—also go up to caution mountain bikers to slow. But newts know no boundaries, and if the rains come in October, they begin to plod before the cars are outlawed. I've read of one man who, at six each morning, would ride his bike, like a boy on an early paper route, to see if the newts were shining on the road. To carry them across, in their direction.

Shortly after we met, she and I visited my hometown together. It was early January, and we decided to take a walk one night in the rain. Above the redwoods, we came to a small, lush meadow where the jeep tracks ran with rivulets and newts. Extrapolating from our flashlight beams, thousands lay in the dark wetness. Trying to find each other. Pacing with cinnamon eyes. My approach was to examine the patch where my foot would fall and then move forward confidently. But further up the hill, when I looked back, there she was, frozen, scanning the ground around her as if a newt might dash under her boot and she could never forgive herself. I had to go back and retrieve her, take her hand, convince her that the newts would survive.

More recently, but years ago now, we lived off the grid in the woods of Oregon for several seasons. We were still young in our relationship then, younger. She painted each day and I made attempts at writing, often staying up late into the night by the thrumming woodstove. Not far up the hill from our meadow was an artificial pond where *Taricha* newts swam lazily along the weedy edge. These were the California newt's closest cousin, the rough-skinned newt, *granulosa*. When both species enter their breeding waters, their skin becomes smooth, losing its warty texture. Their tails grow long and thin to serve as a propeller and rudder. They glide in casual circles and dive into the muck ahead of their corkscrewing tails. Looking down from the bank into the pond, we thought them like bathers in a park.

We swam in the pond on the hottest days and, as caretakers, once we waded in and tore out the sharp aquatic grass around its edge. Occasionally we would see a couple in the shallows in "amplexus," a word that means "an embrace." He grasping her from behind, rubbing her snout with a gland below his chin. They drift together untethered. The male develops "nuptial pads," which look like black thimbles on his sixteen fingers, to improve his chances of holding on to her. For she might squirm away, never to be seen again. We had missed the season, but, earlier in the spring, wild clusters of newts can be found, a mass of males all competing for a single female somewhere in the slimy fray.

The pond was decades old and originally subsidized by the Forest Service so that, in case of wildfire, one of their helicopters could dip a massive bucket on a chain and swing up with water. All those years, the water had only ever fed the homestead's garden; our tomatoes were nurtured by the newts' algal pool. But last summer, the steep drainages finally burned, over a hundred thousand acres across the river. The river canyon, as we knew and came to admire it, was revised in a week's time. The cabin hillside was spared, but I am left imagining newts by the hundreds raining into the fir below the whirring blades, beside each other: their bellies the color of the conflagration, their movement in free fall a kind of slow flame.

Acknowledgments

Many thanks to the publications in which some of these essays previously appeared:

The Threepenny Review: "Chiton" (2015)
Ninth Letter: "The Book of Agate" (2014)
Kenyon Review: "The Afterlife" (2016)
The Southern Review: "Discovering Anna" (2015)
Fourth Genre: "Gone Rogue, or Suck It Up" (2016)
River Teeth: "A Guide to Coyote Management" (2010)
Orion: "The Garden of Earthly Delights" (2016)
Passages North: "Chanty" (2016)
Harvard Review Online: "Slow Flame" (2014)

Thanks also to Ander Monson and New Michigan Press for publishing "Chiton," "Discovering Anna," "A Guide to Coyote Management," "Slow Flame," and one other essay as the chapbook *Chiton, and Other Creatures* (2015), a handsome antecedent to this volume.

I've been blessed with many wonderful teachers over the years. Thanks in particular to: Catherine Imbriglio, Barton St. Armand, and Thalia Field at Brown University; Scott Slovic, Michael P. Branch, Cheryll Glotfelty, and Christopher Coake at the unique Literature and Environment Program at the University of Nevada, Reno; Louise DeSalvo, Kathryn Harrison, and Alexandra Styron at Hunter College. Six of these essays had their start at the Columbia University Writing Program, and I owe a debt to its nonfiction faculty. Special thanks to Amy Benson, Stephen O'Connor, Phillip Lopate, Patricia O'Toole, and James Richardson, who provided insightful feedback on earlier versions of these wanderings. And to Emily Nemens at *The Southern Review* for her attention to "Discovering Anna."

Heartfelt thanks to my many encouraging friends, including Rainer Lee and Wei Tchou, my comrades at Hunter and loyal readers. I am grateful also to the editors at *High Country News* for inducting me into their journalism boot camp after my stint above the Rogue River. Paonia is where the ideas for "The Afterlife" and "The Carcass Toss" were first hatched.

Thanks to the Cow Creek Band of Umpqua Tribe of Indians for hosting me at their moving powwow; to David Pease at the Cole Rivers Hatchery for fielding my questions and giving me a tour; to Chuck Fustish for having me along for the toss; and to Bob, Jason, and Ray for handing me the regulator. Thanks also to Christopher Clark for lending his photo of a diving Anna's; to Kay Atwood, the author of *Illahe: The Story of the Settlement of the Rogue Canyon*; and to all the researchers and writers whose work I borrowed from to produce this collection.

Great thanks to the John Burroughs Association for recognizing "The Book of Agate" with the 2015 John Burroughs Nature Essay Award. Thanks as well to the UC Berkeley-11th Hour Food and Farming Journalism Fellowship, which helped me write "The Carcass Toss"; and to the Djerassi Resident Artists Program, where I finished "The Afterlife" with a view to the ocean from the Middlebrook Studios. And my deep thanks to the PEN Northwest Margery Davis Boyden Wilderness Writing Residency and the Sitka Center for Art and Ecology for long-term residencies and their unbelievable landscapes. The Dutch Henry Homestead introduced me to southern Oregon. Three of these pieces later came to life at the Sitka Center below magical Cascade Head. Bradley, Frank, and Jane Boyden have made an immense contribution to the arts of the Pacific Northwest, and their creativity and generosity are much appreciated.

Thanks in addition to John Daniel for selecting me for the Boyden Residency. He has set a high bar—the gold standard—for writing about the Homestead. He also put me in touch with Jack Shoemaker, and in turn my thanks goes to Jack and the staff at Counterpoint for believing in this book and making it a beautiful, layered reality.

Mountains of thanks to my supportive extended family, including my late grandparents Betty, Bob, Ralph, and Virginia, and my inspiring siblings, Lucy and Simon, who are fellow outdoor enthusiasts.

Much of this book belongs to my wife and most eager reader, Sarah, as I hope these essays make clear.

Finally, thanks to my parents, Holly and Kirk. Since I was small, they've nurtured my love for specimens and creatures with trips into the backyard and to far-flung places. More recently these specimens and creatures have included essays. Their generosity and intelligence have meant the glorious world.

Author photograph by Sarah Bird

ABOUT THE AUTHOR

NICK NEELY grew up south of San Francisco, in the oak and chaparral on the bay side of the Santa Cruz Mountains. He holds an M.A. in Literature and Environment from the University of Nevada, Reno, and M.F.A.s in nonfiction and poetry from Hunter College and Columbia University. His nonfiction has appeared in magazines such as *Orion*, *Audubon*, *Mother Jones*, *High Country News*, *Kenyon Review*, *The Threepenny Review*, *The Georgia Review*, and *Ecotone*. He is a recipient of PEN Northwest's Margery Davis Boyden Wilderness Writing Residency, a UC Berkeley–11th Hour Food and Farming Journalism Fellowship, and the 2015 John Burroughs Nature Essay Award. He lives in Hailey, Idaho, with his wife, the painter Sarah Bird.